SIGHTING BY EYE

Flat Hammock Press
5 Church Street
Mystic, CT 06355
(860) 572-2722; www.flathammockpress.com

All rights reserved. No part of this book may be reproduced or transmitted in any form without written consent of the publisher.

Copyright © 2006 Jim Wesolowski
Introduction © 2006 Stephen Jones
Illustrations Copyright © James A. Mitchell

Library of Congress Cataloging-in-Publication Data

Wesolowski, Jim.
  Sighting by eye : selected essays of a ruminative stonemason / by Jim Wesolowski.
    p. cm.
  ISBN 0-9773725-3-7
  1. Wesolowski, Jim--Anecdotes. 2. Connecticut--Biography--Anecdotes. I. Title.
  CT275.W3888A3 2006
  974.6'0430922--dc22
                           2006022901

ISBN: 0-9773725-3-7

10 9 8 7 6 5 4 3 2 1

Printed in U.S.A.

SIGHTING BY EYE

SELECTED ESSAYS OF A RUMINATIVE STONEMASON

By Jim Wesolowski

Introduction by Stephen Jones
Illustrated by James A. Mitchell

FLAT HAMMOCK PRESS
MYSTIC, CONNECTICUT

Acknowledgments

To my wife Lori and sons Alex and Adam,
three lights in my life that I steer by.
And to Steve Jones for his long-standing
encouragement in word and deed.

Contents

Simplicity

You Can't Take It With You, Not Even a Schwinn 3

The Case for a Good Fitting Shovel 5

Setting the Standard for What a Truck Can Be 7

Nothing Like the Roar of a Vermont Tin Roof 9

The Code of Silence Is One You Shouldn't Break 12

Beauty Without the Option Package 15

Mechanics, Doctors, and Diagnosis 17

The Virtues of Being Thin 19

Connectedness

Five Out of the "Six Hundred and Twelve" 23

Finding Yourself in the Northeast Kingdom 25

Something to Write Home About 29

Maybe What Littering Is All About 31

Separated by a Cell Phone and a Common Language 33

Getting Into the Zone and Getting Away With It 35

Primitive Cultures Would Know What This Rain Meant 37

Discovery

Mastering the Universe on the Rolling Pequot Hills 41

A Fundamental Entity of Nature Gone Wild 43

Fishing Is More Scientific Than Ever 45

In Search of a Body of Water Somewhere Near 47

The Wisdom of Chickens and Their Shepherds 49

Building a Tree House for the Child Inside 51

Looking for Water in all the Wrong Places 53

The World Through the Outhouse Door 57

It's Primarily a Mental Phenomenon 59

A Tradition of Getting Away From It All 61

Rebellion

Inside a Florida Maximum Security Unit 67
When Fast and Furious Meet the Old Dirt Track 69
Grass Is a Habit Worth Breaking 72
Rebellion 75
On the Cutting Edge of Renewable Energy 77
Naming Names 79
The Difficulties in Coming to a Complete Stop 81
Definitely Something About Mary 84

Civilization

Running with the Volvo Crowd Has Its Price 89
Life With the Boring Parts Left Out 91
Maine: The Way Life Was Until You Came 93
Digging into Our Gardening Roots 97
The Poor Get Poorer and the Rich Get Horses 99
Hanging Outside the Gallery 102
No One is Standing by the Old Standbys 104

Mortality

A Teacher Wherever You Find Him 109
You Can't Fish in the Same Ocean Twice 111
A Little Landscaping for the Soul 115
A Game for the Ages on the Fenway 117
Losing Lieutenant Morrow 120
Passing Through Some Deep Uncharted Place 123
Knowing What Boat to Choose 125
Some of the Ties That Bind Us 128

Introduction

By Stephen Jones

Of all the essays Jim Wesolowski has fashioned, I think his piece in the spring of 2005 about the well-made shovel best exemplifies both his message and his method. He begins by finding an old tool in the cellar of a house where he is working. He has completed the more skillful part of his job and is now merely doing what my scientist colleagues call so dismissively "scut work." He is doing what so few in our culture do, let alone celebrate; he is cleaning up after himself. In the expediency of grabbing the first instrument at hand, he makes a discovery:

"I was pleasantly surprised. It was heavy at the business end, but the overall balance of the tool made that weight work for me. The design was such that my hands worked in a kind of easy churning motion when I wielded its compact form. It was a flat shovel and there was a lot of force brought to bear at the cutting edge. It scooped up broken glass and other debris on the asphalt parking lot like it was made for just that purpose."

Never one to let the beginning of an insight die with its first flash, Jim, the workman, maintains his focus: "But something else caught my attention about the shovel. I felt as though it was made to fit into my hands." Characteristically he takes the shock of recognition to the next stage: "I have noticed this about some of my old tools;" and then the marvelous phrase-making, "they seem more at home to the touch."

From there he goes into a comparison with contemporary tools that "seem big and clunky to hold and use" and moves further to the larger idea, musing "as if one size fits all and yet fits no one in particular."

As the piece continues we follow Jim as his curiosity leads him to attempt to account for what has so "pleasantly surprised" him. He interviews a friend who adds an anecdote about an oysterman's shovel on a dark night and a bit of reading from a man who does welded sculpture. This sculptor extends Jim

vii

into considering the tools we carry about as parts of our body such as our teeth and, "You know the old wives' tales about how a bad bite can lead to all kinds of ruin, from headaches to a stutter." Moving from the folk wisdom of the past, he drops casually a modern civic note: "What could our lousy tools be doing to us?"

Before he gets carried away with the social implications of bad tools, he backs off to a thorough, yet marvelously readable examination of two of those old tools that do the job. The first is a ball-peen hammer that he picked up at an estate sale; the second is a big wrench he inherited from his pipe-fitter father. He concludes that the wrench is:

"By today's standards … a work of art, made by a human hand for a human hand. And like the shovel, a little of the mystery of its making rubs off on what it is used to make, which is the measure of a good tool."

It is not that Jim feels he must hang onto everything in the past. His piece about the bicycle he finds while he's on a Block Island vacation with his wife and two sons is a marvelous excursion in taking advantage of the moment and then knowing when to let go.

I first met Jim some twenty years ago when he was sitting in one of my classes at the University of Connecticut at Avery Point. The characteristic look on his face was that of the furrowed brow. Things that other students just shrugged off, puzzled him. His written responses bore the syntactical equivalent of the furrowed brow, and before he grew into his craft these sentences sometimes also produced the furrowed brow on his reader. At one point he wanted to write a novel about Polish expatriates. I think that in self-defense I threw something by Conrad at him. We have not discussed the expatriate novel for some time. In the meantime we have these wonderful forays about the local land. Jim's father was not only a pipe fitter, but for most of Jim's life owned a Christmas tree farm in the upper valley of the Mystic River watershed. His mother seems to have also been what used to be described as "salt of the earth."

It's been years since I've actually watched Jim put words together on the page, but I have been privileged to observe him work in a variety of trades, each of which he has helped me see as a metaphor for writing. Perhaps my most enduring image of Jim putting together something of higher worth out of the detritus of found life was when he was rebuilding a wall at the West Mystic Wooden Boat Company. The drill was that he had to use only the rocks that were *in situ*. Furthermore, he was using no mortar. Each rock had to fit on its own. One day it was especially foggy, an effect that isolated Jim

Introduction

from the harbor and eventually air brushed out all of the boatyard except the immediate pile of rocks from which he was composing his wall. His silhouette took on an epic aura, as if here was the first true man on earth building order out of chaos, slowly, but surely. And that's how Jim builds his essays on contemporary civilization: not out of the rant of political slogans or the gobbledygook of psycho-babble, but from the ground up, word by carefully chosen word; dry walls that need no facile cement to hold them in place because it is as if each word had been made to fit his hands.

Stephen Jones
Schooner Wharf
Mystic, Connecticut

"Our minds becoming ruminative, we find a calm delight ..."
—Horace Smith, 1841

"They lift huge stone blocks with almost supernatural ease. They can match a stone with a gap, a gap with a stone, with an easy measuring glance. If there is one ancient craft that has survived here into modern times unimpaired, even enhanced, it is the art of dry-stone walling ..."
—Jan Morris, *A Writer's House in Wales*

"The fish trap exists because of the fish; once you've gotten the fish, you can forget the trap. The rabbit snare exists because of the rabbit; once you've gotten the rabbit, you can forget the snare. Words exist because of meaning; once you've gotten the meaning, you can forget the words. Where can I find a man who has forgotten words so I can have a word with him?"
—Chuang-Tzu
4th Century B.C.E. Taoist sage

"I think over again my small adventures, my fears. Those small ones that seemed so big, for all the vital things I had to get and reach; and yet there is only one great thing. The only thing, to live to see the great day that dawns and the light that fills the world."
—19th Century Inuit Native American

Foreword

I have always liked Ilse Aichinger's allegory, "The Bound Man." In it a man wakes up one day to find himself tied hand to foot. But he learns to master his life within the limits of his rope and goes on to join a circus and become famous for feats of physical prowess, none more renowned than his encounter with a wild animal:

"He stopped. The animal came towards him though the thinning foliage. He could make out its shape, the slant of its neck, its tail which swept the ground, and its receding head. If he had not been bound, perhaps he would have tried to run away, but as it was he did not even feel fear. He stood calmly with dangling arms and looked down at the wolf's bristling coat, under which the muscles played like his own underneath the rope. He thought the evening wind was still between him and the wolf when the beast sprang. The man took care to obey his rope."

I have not always been successful in obeying my rope, but I have tried.

If we live long enough we all learn that there is at least one room, one place within our being that we are strong, almost invincible. A runner feels it in his pace, a martial artist in his balance, a marksman in his breath. You leave this place at your peril, but within it the gods move with you stride for stride and keep you company.

I know some, perhaps most, writers like words. They love sentences, paragraphs. I suppose I do too, but even more, I love what the writing tells. I love how it has a chance to move and incite. I think that moving another mind by making it think, by sharing consciousness, by opening another and yourself to the known and the unknown; and maybe even a glance toward the unknowable … this is the writer's work and the writer's joy.

All 48 of the essays in this volume were written as newspaper columns over the past 15 years. In a way they are a loose-knit diary of my life during that time.

Sighting By Eye

This diary aspect did not mean all that much to me until recently when I was trying to recall the details of a trip one of my sons and I had taken north to Vermont one summer. Suddenly I remembered I had written a column about it and it all came rushing back.

I can not tell you how pleased I am that the adventure we shared together would be preserved in this book, among others, and for so long as the paper and binding last, he and others might look back and find memories within its covers.

Throughout life we sometimes wish we had kept a journal of all the common, day-to-day things we did along the way. The monumental items in life are etched in our minds, but the little joys and wonders we hold so dear are swept away in the blink of an eye.

I have written about my own experiences here. I plead the same case as Thoreau, when he said he wrote about his own life because he knew no other subject as well. I concur. I have tried to write about life not as it has struck me alone, but as it strikes the humanity in all of us.

When I told a friend in 1989 that I was going to start writing a column so that I could record the world as it happened around me, he laughed.

But I wrote it anyway, bound by what, I can not say.

For most of the years I wrote this column I wrote it every other week. It seemed like a good interval. The interval was sufficient to leave me feeling fresh between times, and yet often enough to keep a comfortable rhythm. But for the last few years I went on a once-every-third-week schedule.

At first this change was disquieting. It felt as if the column was lost and then found again new, jagged and rough, each time. Ideas that came to me on a cyclic basis generated by a strange internal momentum—as in bodies in motion stay in motion—seemed to slip away. Like a top that does not spin fast enough, it begins to wobble. I wobbled and could not find my tempo. It may not have shown much on the outside, but on the inside was turmoil.

Gradually though, the three-week gestation began to suit me. It had to. This occurred about the same time in my early fifties that my physical powers as a stonemason began to wane. I watched as my ability to perform fell short of my desire to build. But having no choice but to complain or adapt, I complained plenty and then made some adjustments.

I have found that when you build fewer stonewalls you think more about every stone you place in them. I notice individual stones more now. They pass through my hands more slowly. I put them into the wall with the knowledge that there is an end in sight to the work. As more aches and pains visit my body as toll for each stone lifted past and present, the stone I reach for now is more than just an irascible object with which to wiggle and shape for filling a hole in a wall—it is my reason for being. The stone and I are falling into the wall together: Wrestlers connected in a landscape ruled by gravity and time.

Foreword

Likewise, my interrupted columns have become a rhythm unto themselves. We are all interrupted eventually and permanently. I see these essays now not as short writing assignments for pay, but as a journal of time shared. I see them as a letter I would write to my sons. I would send these jottings, these notes of our lives, not as instruction or advice, but as memory of having traveled the road together.

May 06 —JJW

Simplicity

Sighting By Eye

Simplicity

You Can't Take It With You, Not Even a Schwinn

The last time I saw the Schwinn it was sitting next to the back door of a Block Island tavern where I had carefully, almost lovingly, placed it the day before.

Our star-crossed paths had intersected for a brief time and now we were parting strangers again. As I watched it disappear from view on my way to the ferry dock, I had no regrets.

Strangely, the Schwinn had come to dominate my week-long stay on Block Island. It was the way I transported my body to and fro for six days, but it also became a vehicle for moving the mind during my time on the island. It was a rusty, rickety prism to see the world from and through.

It began the second day while I was literally on my way to rent a bicycle.

On a chance glance over the embankment on Ocean Avenue I spied a wreck of a bike in a narrow three-foot strip of tidal grass. I climbed down to sea level. While my wife shuddered on the sidewalk above—not because of any physical danger to me, but because of threat to her reputation—I weighed the issue.

A list of maladies included: front wheel detached; handlebars reversed to 180-degrees normal; pedals that would not turn; various stickers hanging off; a bright orange patina of oxidation on formerly white wheels; chrome fenders encrusted with deep-pitted rust; and, for good measure, a seagull feather stuck to the frame. A real beauty.

I looked back up towards my wife for moral support at that pivotal moment, but she was looking the other way like she didn't know me.

Yet another tug at the pedals made them move with surprising smoothness. The front wheel looked as if it could be reunited. I steeled myself for the effort and staggered up the bank with what had to be 40-plus pounds of Eisenhower-era iron.

With borrowed tool kit, can of oil, elbow grease, and a little help, the Schwinn came back together and drove quite well for a bike pushing 50.

3

Sighting By Eye

As I rode up and down the little hills of Block Island I began to marvel at what such a simple machine could do. The bike was one-speed and so elemental it evoked the feel of a hand tool as opposed to a new-fangled power tool. It made new bikes look trivial, ephemeral, footnotes. It represented that first giant leap of personal wheeled transport after the ox cart. Alas, it was the distant precursor, albeit un-powered, of the famed SUV. After all, many of the original baby boomers had cut their teeth on Schwinns. My own first bike at age six was a cousin to this very model.

The bike was a great conversation starter and with the right kind of people, I noticed.

The smug wouldn't look at me, except to perhaps grimace or whisper under their breath. But I didn't mind filtering them out to begin with. Those with a sense of humor, a gusto for life, a screw untightened somewhere in their evolving psyche, for these it was a magnet.

A crusty taxi driver would slow down and across her front seat hurl a compliment. I would pick out a stranger's voice a 100 feet away, "that's quite a bike you have there."

A young couple from New York noticed my ride outside a restaurant and we exchanged pleasantries. They, it seemed, were driving their own seasoned peddlers, she a 1949 Elgin and he a 60s-something BSA. She blew her Elgin's little battery-powered horn to cap the moment.

The landlady at the cottage where we stayed marveled at how it could go the two miles each way to town every day. The other three members of my family had modern bicycles with a total of 63 gears between them, but I always seemed to get to town at about the same time, sometimes before them.

All went well, until one afternoon outside the island's grocery a fellow stopped short.

"That looks just like Captain Nick's bike," he said.

He came over and fingered a tattered sticker on the fender. He looked up and said, "Where did you get it?"

I told him straight off, "down the road in a pile of junk at water's edge."

Deep in thought he scratched his head and walked away.

I began inquiring after the possible owner. I went to look for him, and on the third attempt, the day before our departure, I found an acquaintance of the man in question. He laughed a deep belly laugh when I told him about the bike. He told me, keep it, the Captain hadn't ridden a bike in years. But I insisted I wanted to leave it on the island for someone else to use. So he told me to leave it by the back door and he'd see to it.

Taken home, that bike would be a rusty relic; left behind, a pleasant memory.

Simplicity

The Case for a Good Fitting Shovel

We found an old shovel in a Noank basement recently while we were straightening up. It had a wooden handle with a place to fit your hand, and it was riveted and reinforced in a way I hadn't seen before. It could have been down in that basement for 100 years.

We saved it, and later in the week I had occasion to need a shovel and grabbed it. I was pleasantly surprised. It was heavy at the business end, but the overall balance of the tool made that weight work for me like a breeze. The design was such that my hands worked in a kind of easy churning motion when I wielded its compact form. It was a flat shovel and there was a lot of force brought to bear at the cutting edge. It scooped up broken glass and other debris on the asphalt parking lot like it was made for just that purpose.

But something else caught my attention about the shovel. It felt like it was made to fit into my hands. I have noticed this about some of my old tools; they seem more at home to the touch. Other tools seem big and clunky to hold and use, as if one size fits all and fits no one in particular. You feel like you are adapting to the tool rather than the other way round. Most of my tools are this way; after you use them for a while you get accustomed to them—they become comfortable by association only and you never know the difference, except when a tool like this shovel comes along.

When I told this to a friend he

mentioned something about how in the old days oystermen working in the dark were able to instantly tell if they had the right shovel by the way it felt in their hands.

Walking in from my shed the other day it struck me that perhaps for generations now we have not known this kind of closeness to our hand tools. At first glance this may seem inconsequential, but I am inclined to say there is more to this than first meets the eye, or hand.

Nathan Cabot Hale in his book, *Creating Welded Sculpture*, points out how good sculptors develop "an acute awareness of the anatomical basis of tool design." He maintains that all hand tools really are an extension of the functions embodied in the human hands, teeth, and jaws. And I guess I'd know pretty quickly if one of my teeth were out of alignment. After a while we may learn to put up with it, but that misalignment will end up exacting its toll, causing some kind of stress somewhere in our lives. You know the old wives' tale about how a bad bite can lead to all kinds of ruin, from headaches to a stutter. What could our lousy tools be doing to us?

I have a ball-peen hammer that came from an estate sale which I would date to the mid to late 1800s. It has a long, slender wooden handle that goes from about an inch and a half in diameter at the butt end to less than half an inch toward the hammer's head where it thickens again. It has a sort of elongated hour-glass form and an inordinately long handle compared to anything I have seen in modern hammers. To hold it is to know that it was made to have fingers wrapped around it and to strike with surprising force and precision.

A tool that I inherited from my father's barn probably dates from late 18th to early 19th century. It looks like a giant pipe wrench, but its jaws stay square and it is just over three feet long. To adjust the wrench one has to loosen a metal wedge and then drive it in again. This wrench weighs 12 pounds, but it fits into the hands and balances so well it barely seems to weigh five. One glance tells you it was hand-forged, and though it is handsome to behold, none of its lines has the perfect symmetry of a mass-produced tool.

By today's standards it is a work of art, made by a human hand for a human hand. And like that shovel, a little of the mystery of its making rubs off on what it is used to make, which is the measure of a good tool.

Simplicity

Setting the Standard for What a Truck Can Be

I had seen the little pickup truck parked idle for about ten years. The only movement I perceived about it was the comings and goings of wasps in the driver's-side fender in summer and the rise and fall of snow on the hood in winter. The VW pickup sat outside at the south-facing end of an abandoned building in a rural setting whose exact location I think it better not to divulge.

All this was a pleasant diversion until recently, when a desire came over me to find a more fuel efficient vehicle. Then a series of heretical "what-ifs" way outside mainstream parameters pressed in on me. What if it could be made to run? What if it wasn't as rusted as it should be after all these years? What if such a Spartan vehicle could be used unashamedly as transport in an era when windshield wipers think for us and turn on by their own authority?

Rockwell Kent, in his book *Wilderness*, talks of our potential of being "less products of a culture than makers of it." So I resolved to try the road less traveled on the gas-guzzling freeway (why do they call it free when there is nothing free about it) and resurrect this midget of a truck with its diminutive 4-cylinder motor and 13-inch wheels.

I knew at some subconscious level that driving small cars and trucks was possible. After all, I had traveled to other parts of the world and with my own eyes had seen the successful use of tiny vehicles to conduct various forms of business without difficulty. In the past, my ethnocentrically-fueled attitudes had pitied those poor unfortunates in their mobile sardine cans riding on the edge of certain disaster.

Three fuel pumps, one oil change, one fuel distributor, three fuel filters, a gas tank, fuel line, four spark plugs, various light electrical fuses and relays, new tires (they were a gift) and perhaps 30 hours of labor and countless hours of worry later—I think I know what disaster is. But I also know there is something called hope.

7

Sighting By Eye

After flailing along for weeks studying repair manuals and asking practically everyone for advice, nothing seemed to work. The best I could do was get the motor to idle, but it would stall if you touched the gas pedal. Ron, my friend from Vermont, visited and viewed the inside of the engine compartment like one would view the inside of a coffin during a wake—with respect and dread. Apparently undaunted or unable to let his reputation sag, he whipped out the small adjustable wrench he carries everywhere with him and made a few adjustments. He tugged on a few wires and hovered over the engine while it sputtered, starved for fuel, or air, or both. I know it had spark, because I got a nice solid shock during the course of my investigation. He left me with his condolences and a shop manual big enough to ballast a small sailboat with.

Finally, I caved in and brought the truck to Budzecks in Norwich. They seemed to have an understanding of what I was going through, and they certainly had a much better understanding of what was going on with the vehicle. They have no waiting room, no free coffee, and no internet connections for waylaid foreign car owners. They do not coddle their customers, but they do try to fix your car—which is the only thing I had hoped to be paying for. Four-hundred dollars later they had it running and driving. I took it home on a flatbed trailer in triumph and drove it around my yard for about 15 minutes before it died.

I left it in the yard and could hardly bear to look at it through the window. But the next day, once the shock of abject failure and defeat had worn off, new plots on how to fix it filtered in. The Budzecks were consulted. After an hour of primitive diagnostic work I found a small fuse needed replacing.

Today I was out driving around my yard again, saving a truck and a planet at the same time.

Simplicity

Nothing Like the Roar of a Vermont Tin Roof

We called it "camping out" and we did it on the fresh cut hay field nestled along the far hill at the northeast boundary of our farm in Old Mystic. We had nothing over our heads but the stars. We would lose half the night talking as 11-year-olds do and wake with a fine coat of dew upon us.

To prepare our camping spot we would drag the old rotary mower up the hill, pace out an area, and cut short the tall timothy grass at the woods' edge. There is no other smell like tall field grass cut so close to the ground. I can not describe it except to say that it is nothing like the smell of a domesticated lawn, which is paltry in comparison. One whiff of it, which I smell by accident once or twice a decade now, brings me back to my sleeping bag and hay field.

So when I took my youngest son camping to Vermont recently I suppose I was looking for some such bookmark of the senses to hold the memory hard against the long haul of time which marches on.

The moments I captured first on this new trip were splitting white birch firewood at dusk at our campsite just outside Island Pond. And then there was being eaten alive as the two of us worked feverishly to put up our tent while mosquitoes attacked from all sides in the gathering darkness. Swatting, cussing, sweating, we beat them away, survived the battle, and crawled safe inside.

The second night we went to our friend's cabin near Lake Willoughby. It is a small 12-by-14-foot, one-room affair, tucked far in the woods with two bunks and a wood stove which was not needed in the sweltering July heat. We endured the coming and goings of mice on the rafters above our heads and the faint aroma of a gas generator that had been stored there and recently removed. I had thought not to stay inside at all and set our tent outside where we could again enjoy the "wilderness" as it were. But the forecast was for a thunderstorm to come sweeping across upper New York state and slice

9

Sighting By Eye

Simplicity

across northern Vermont. My host and friend Ron shook his head. "You're better off to stay inside," he said. "It could get pretty crazy."

But the sky looked fine and Ron, my boy and I sat around a fire outside the cabin till late. Finally, Ron walked down the dirt road to his house and we two lay in our bunks, me on the bottom tier and my son on the top, and watched his DVD player until its batteries quit. After saying goodnight, we closed our eyes and listened to the lonely quiet that is particular to the northern Vermont woods. It is a quiet that penetrates all your defenses.

I awoke startled, face down in the darkness. A deafening roar filled my ears. It was like being inside a 55-gallon metal drum pelted by a hail of falling rock. I would never have believed the downpour of rain would be so loud on the cabin's metal roof.

I had to yell at the top of my lungs to get the attention of my son in the bunk above. He answered in a tone that told me he wasn't too afraid, so I let him be. I kept still and pushed my face into the top of the sleeping bag. I looked at the luminous dial of my watch, which read 1:45 a.m.

For a full 40 minutes the roar went on unabated. Lightning flashes showed through the screen windows and the pane of glass in the door. It was a longer performance than I had seen on any Independence Day. The wind whipped the trees wildly outside and I wondered if the tiny cabin, which had been built elsewhere and dragged to the site by a bulldozer, would be thrown off its moorings. But it held.

In the morning we slept late and woke to the hushed green woods around the cabin. The dirt track to our dooryard was muddy, and we barely got the car out. I hung my head out the car window around the sharp corner on the logging road and a sticky black mud sprayed on me and the seat back.

The storm had broken the humid spell we'd been having, at least in the north woods, and the air was ring-in-a-bell clear and cool. We packed up our gear and, after saying our goodbye to Ron, headed home. The ephemeral summer had slipped away without our knowing it. Years go by before we understand and can mark the endpoint of life's sweet chapters. While we live it we know next to nothing.

In the memory's inventory, a new item had taken a place in the camping section, alongside the smell of fresh cut hay. It was the sound of one Vermont tin roof clapping.

The Code of Silence is One You Shouldn't Break

After I disconnected my car battery last month to clean the positive and negative terminals my life changed for the better.

Some might say the results were mixed, some positive, some negative, but I disagree.

The battery looked great, but inside the car there was trouble. The temperature was now default set to Celsius and the clock ran on 24-hour military time. But the real problem was the radio, which no longer worked.

I recall the old rock and roll anthem with the lyrics: "sign says you got to have a membership card to get inside" My radio proudly displayed the word "CODE" in big letters across its read-out screen and in its computerized ignorance refused to negotiate. In the 30-mile-each-way commute to work, my radio, once a familiar and constant if noisy companion now stared silently at me espousing the word "CODE" like some friend that demanded an apology before he would take me back.

The car dealer service guy, evidently cut from the same cloth as the radio, was also impatient and rigid in his interpretation of my plight. I had no sooner mentioned that I had disconnected the batt… than he cut me off and said: "You need the radio code" Yeah, as a matter of fact I did.

At that point he tried to determine if I was the true owner of my car over the phone. Had they ever done work on my car? "No," I said. I did not tell him I would not trust him with my car at the rates his dealership charges. I told him they had worked on my wife's car, which is a Swedish cousin to mine. I gave her name and particulars. Begrudgingly he then requested the VIN number and finally in a tone which said he was bestowing the DaVinci Code on me, spoke the number sequence "6-2-3-6."

There, I had it. But I could not use it because I had already in a weak moment of frenzied frustration tried to break the code myself and the radio had totally locked up. So now, following a witches' menu of bat's wing and eye of newt ground to a powdery dust like my patience, I obeyed the tedious

Simplicity

steps and left the ignition on for two hours to do my penance so that my radio would respond to my car's personal code.

And it did not work.

I waited a few days, trying to forget the whole matter, and hummed on my way to work. I started to think about things while I drove my car—the meaning of life, the futility of war. I even came up with a reverse acronym for SUV as one sped by me while the driver sipped coffee and probably listened to her radio: Such Ugly Vehicles. I began to hear the clinking sound of my tools rattling together in the back of my car making their own tiny chorus of encouragement. There was the soft sound of the wind whishing by. The trees were green and lush outside and spring had arrived. I was awakening from something, I didn't know what.

Occasionally though, I would reach for the radio button like I suppose an ex-smoker reaches for a pack of cigarettes in what is now a smoke-free pocket. Then I would reach again a few moments later without thinking.

I called the same dealer again and spoke to the same service guy.

After I told him what happened—nothing—he told me without explanation or apology that I would have to bring the car into the dealership. I thought it was more of his not believing I owned the car, when he cut me off in his I-know-what's-going-on-before-you-ask-it-manner, and said, "The radio must have been replaced." I thanked him and told him I would think about it.

Sighting By Eye

Last week I mentioned to my two sons that the radio didn't work and the dealer's code didn't match. "Don't you remember the guy you bought the car from pulled out the radio and showed us the code?" one of them said. I had no idea.

While I watched they pulled out the radio and written on top were the numbers "6-3-3-3." With a faint hint of reservation, knowing something good was about to end, I did not interfere as my oldest son followed some ancient rite of compliance and conformity that makes the world turn and entered the code.

The radio flared up, peace in my lifetime had come to an end.

Simplicity

Beauty Without the Option Package

I stood in front of the barn's new skeleton, taking in a building that in the morning sun looked more like a cathedral than a barn. The bare timbers shone clean and fresh, strong and true.

The Amish builders were missing on Sunday, so today the new structure was quiet—as if it too were resting—exhausted at its birth in just two days. Its midwives do not work on the Sabbath, I am told.

But the memory of their hammers' ring still resonates. No fancy nailer guns with their zump-zump sounds were used here. All day that Friday and Saturday on this hillside in Franklin, the Amish men and boys plied their trade in a way that reminded me of prayer: constant and confident. Plain shirts and black pants, held by thin, dark suspenders. A straw hat, black sneakers, long sleeves rolled part way up the forearm. Slight, wiry men, agile on the rafters and joists, deceptive in their strength. Their leader, a man in his 30s with a narrow beard that traversed the rim of his chin.

Their movements were governed by the essential. They came seasoned and prepared for their work like their truck-load of wood. The timbers were marked and notched beforehand. The builders found their way through the new barn as they built it, board by board, nail by nail, beam by beam. It reminded me of making a road as you traveled it—without missing a step along the way.

We have come to associate beauty with window dressing. We even claim it a necessity. I am afraid that options and frills are indispensable to life. Everything must be sexy in design and jazzed up in nature. Pickup trucks, for instance, are no longer principally designed for work, but for flashing around town in, oozing machismo. Form not following function, but a slave to the pitch man's whim. Everything must be made to sell, not to last.

Thus I smile at the thought of the Amish modesty as I saw it that weekend and how it must appear to the mind of the average Madison Avenue-saturated citizen. How he must think the Amish are missing out on so much that is

15

Sighting By Eye

wonderful in life with all his self-imposed simplicity. But from my observation of that barn and its builders, I don't think they're missing that much.

More than 2,500 people were said to have made the pilgrimage to witness this barn-raising. From what I saw, many seemed to yearn for something intangible as they watched this simple creation build toward the sky.

Simplicity

Mechanics, Doctors, and Diagnosis

If my Vermont mechanic friend Ron was a doctor I would drive the four-and-a-half hours to the Canadian border for an appointment. Instead I call him long distance for practical and insightful advice on truck repair.

I once heard that doctors have become technicians. I'm not surprised when you think about how dependent they and all of us are on machines of one kind or another for diagnostic assistance. The days of the mechanic that listens to your list of complaints and comes up with the right answer are probably over. Both people and automobiles are hooked up to a computer that tells them what's wrong.

But I still believe that in all ventures which involve knowledge and technique there is a point where all method dissolves into a certain innocence in the presence of mystery. These few receptive practitioners perform not so much on a higher level but in a different way—one that pushes their thoughts and actions to the standard of "art."

Through decades of experience my mechanic friend has learned a great deal. His linchpin attribute is his curiosity. And unlike many people expert in his field, he is open to new deviations and truths—this to the point you could call him a blue collar Leonardo or a "jack-of-all-trades," at least in those he has had reason to touch upon. On the occasion of

Sighting By Eye

a recent acquisition of a new old vehicle I called him with a laundry list of ailments. His prowess in understanding the inner workings of a 12-year-old Ford Bronco was stunning. When I told him I had taken out the fuel pump relay and my reasons why, his deadpan remark was, "That's the green one." But I knew that behind that terse remark was the wherewithal to dissect blindfolded the fuel system from gas gauge to gas tank of said vehicle.

When I mentioned the rot in the tailgate and the non-functioning electric window he laid it on the line for me: "You can't open the tailgate until you open the window first." That I had already realized, but as to how I could open the window first, he told me a little story of three wires and a battery charger which could huff and puff and put that window down.

For all his close-mouthed conciseness he never seems to make up his mind before you get out your complete explanation or, in my case, quasi-mechanical babbling. Though I can't see him over the phone, you can bet the wheels are turning in his brain adding up the pros and cons.

And when you tell him something that is contrary to his seasoned opinion, his customary reply is, "Oh yeah?" But that oh yeah is part surprise, part question, and part let's hear more. Once in a while the tone is down an octave and it is a challenge, but rarely.

I've seen a few doctors that work like this too. But as in auto mechanics they are few and far between. You're lucky if you find one and don't lose him or her if you do.

My sense is that the good operators in these two disciplines are listeners. They are not moving at a speed faster than you are, and they adjust their speed if they are. At the moment they are dealing with you it feels like 100 percent of their attention is on what you have to say.

I prefer my doctors and mechanics keep thinking right up to and through their best opinions, always leaving room for more information and possible new determinations.

Far too much emphasis is placed on giving out medicine or installing new parts; in other words, jumping ahead to the solution when the question has not been fully framed. From my teaching days I remember how eager students are to rush headlong to get an answer that does not suit the question. Ultimately it is the question that holds the answer. Fathoming the question reveals the answer like peeling the concentric rings of an onion.

Maybe I should call Vermont and ask Ron for the name of a good doctor. But I can't remember Ron going to a doctor except in an emergency. And of course, it goes without saying; Ron does not go to mechanics.

Simplicity

The Virtues of Being Thin

Over the years, I have not been moved very far by thick books.

It is the thin ones that have succeeded in train-wrecking my psyche, though in a good way.

I have suspected fat books from the start.

Once I learned how hard it was for anyone to come up with something really new to say, I realized that thick books, especially non-fiction, are full of the worst kind of padding. Most of the things they have to say have already, in one form or another, appeared in print somewhere else.

Take the sizzling pot-boiler *The Elements of Style* (85 pages), by William Strunk Jr. and E. B. White. It is a pretty good little handbook on how to put together a sentence. It is clear and well-written. The authors are not trying to impress you with how much they know.

Writing brief is the true indication of a master. Anyone can shovel it on, but few can hone it down. Mark Twain once apologized to a friend for writing such a long letter. He said he "didn't have time to write a short one."

Years ago in school, I gave my students a mandate to write only two typed pages on a subject. They thought it was heresy. Knowing how hard it is to write one good sentence, never mind 10 or 20, I thought it was appropriate. The grumbling in the ranks got so pronounced at one point that I said okay, write as many pages as you want, but I will count only the first two.

An assignment I recently received revived this whole issue. I was told to read a 90-page book called *Experience & Education* by John Dewey.

Sighting By Eye

I can only thank the higher powers that it is brief, because the going is so tough. I imagine it to be the Mount Everest of textbooks. You have to fight tooth and nail with a rock hammer to claim comprehension of a few short pages, only to get pinned down in the worst snowstorm of convoluted sentences I have ever seen. So far, I have read the first 45 pages—half of the book—but I know I will have to read at least the first 30 of those pages again to begin to grasp their meaning.

Yet even so, Dewey, in his great but circuitous wisdom, knew enough to write a thin book.

Considering he was a Ph.D., he must have had a lot of native intelligence.

In closing, I would like to recommend a short list of short reading for the upcoming short summer: *The Forgotten Art of Building a Stone Wall*, (61 pages), *Zen in the Art of Archery*, (81 pages), *Diary of an Early American Boy*, (108 pages), and *The Survival of the Bark Canoe* (114 pages).

Connectedness

Sighting By Eye

Connectedness

Five Out of the "Six Hundred and Twelve"

On what might be the eve of war, I remembered something I had overlooked.

On the Old Mystic Vietnam War Memorial there is a short inscription above five names.

It reads: "To Honor Those Brave Men of The Mystic River Valley Lost in The Vietnam Conflict."

It's a simple, terse statement but it encompasses a broad sweep of American history in this tiny park. There's the stone bench and the stream that runs swiftly by a few yards away. Cars stop and start at the nearby intersection oblivious, and most passersby have no idea of the park or the tale told on the stone nestled there.

The words "Mystic River Valley" caught my eye immediately. There are probably few of us who would describe ourselves as living in a river valley. We usually see ourselves identified with any number of things, but certainly not the landscape that surrounds us.

But from atop a ledge along Lantern Hill Road, decades ago before the trees grew tall, you could see the Main Block in downtown Mystic any day of the week. From that ledge you could also make out the two shoulders of hills heading south along the stream, then the river, and on out to sea. You could also see the flat plain in between those two ridge lines that make what that monument calls the Mystic River Valley.

Geography is a beautiful thing, especially when you realize it binds you to your home. It puts you in a place and in a time, because, as it seems to me, geography is all about time, the interaction of time and earth. That awareness is what some would describe as "spirit of place." One author with a new book out about Native Americans and Gambling told me the other day that he believes the place we come from shapes us, makes us who we are. If you live

23

Sighting By Eye

in Ireland you become Irish, if you live in New England you take on that character, forged by forces seen and unseen in the spirit of the place. When we read that these five men were lost in a faraway conflict, a little piece of us is lost too, if, because of nothing else, by that connection. If we identify with the place then we can identify with those who come from it. They are part of us because they were part of our home.

There was a book published last year titled: *612*. Under the title there is the inscription: "Biographies of the 612 Connecticut men who died in Vietnam. Compiled by the students of Capt. Nathan Hale Middle School, Coventry, Connecticut."

In this book I looked up the five names of those brave men of the Mystic River Valley. They are all there. One of the men is listed as missing in action. Some of the biographies are short, some are longer. But most of them are abbreviated like the lives they chronicle.

Opening that book and walking up to that war memorial feel very much like the same thing, evoking what T.S. Eliot described as "the still point in the turning world." You come close to those fallen soldiers and it is your biography too. We learn when they were born, and when they died. When they entered the service and when they arrived in Vietnam. We also learn their rank, MOS (military occupation specialty)—most were infantry—and where and how they died (explosions, small arms fire, helicopter and plane crashes). The data may seem sparse, but all you have to do to fill in the details is take a breath of fresh air and the magnitude of their sacrifice becomes immediately apparent.

Years ago I listened to Pulitzer Prize-nominated writer Ronald Lee Fleming speak to the Society of the Founders of Norwich. At the close of the evening he put up a slide which read:

"We will preserve only what we love, we love only what we understand, and we understand only what we are taught."

I have not written the names of those five men because they can be seen every day of the week from the river valley they lived in. This much we can teach ourselves.

Connectedness

Finding Yourself in the Northeast Kingdom

It's hard to get a handle on the Northeast Kingdom of Vermont.

I've been going there for years as a replacement for Maine, whose main artery, I-95, is hopelessly clogged with too many cars and too much development.

But what gets in your blood when you spend time in this part of Vermont doesn't register on any of the measuring systems we've calibrated for our rat-race world.

We pulled up to my friend Ron's dooryard about 20 miles south of the Canadian border. It was almost dark, and the small house, a converted summer camp, was deserted. Not even Ron's 150-pound dog, Bruno, was around to snarl at us.

Then off in the distance, up the hill, through the woods, we hear the ring of a hammer. Not since I was a child can I remember anybody working solely by the light of a rising moon. But sure enough, Ron was pounding nails into his latest creation, a giant woodshed, big enough to hold 18 cords of firewood.

Approaching in the semidarkness along one of the logging trails that crisscross Ron's 50 acres, we call out with the salutatory, "Building inspector! You got a permit for that thing."

Ron ceased the hammering and peered down from the bucket of his old International tractor, which he was using as makeshift scaffolding. Though he hadn't seen us since June, and had no idea we were coming, he acted like he'd been expecting us.

Shortly all work stopped, as seems the tradition when visitors come calling in this part of Vermont, and we stood around in the darkness, shadowy figures five feet apart, faces indistinguishable, shooting the chill October breeze.

25

Sighting By Eye

We help Ron unload his pickup truck, which never comes home from work empty, and then we retire to his kitchen table for more talk and a review of the DeLorme topographic atlas we brought along.

Ron pours over the map. His hands are so big they look like two jointed baseball gloves hovering over the tiny blue specks that denote trout ponds.

Finally, he points out a small beaver pond that is supposed to be full of native brookies, "but can't be fished from shore." Mercifully, he knows we have a 1916 Old Town canoe strapped to the roof of the Jeep outside.

We get land directions to the pond and next morning set out bright and early.

I have read that people in the Northeast Kingdom consider where they live as the prime characteristic of their identity. Whereas people from the rest of the country usually define themselves by their career, what they do for a living, these Vermonters base who they are on where they live. Most of us would be in trouble identity-wise if we had to define ourselves by where we happen to live at the moment, going from place to place as we do pursuing "advancement."

By 1:00 p.m., we are exhausted and hungry. We have driven, and tramped

Connectedness

in the woods, and driven and tramped again. We have asked more directions of the few available people we find, but no one can tell us how to find this little No Name Pond. We have long since exhausted Ron's directions, and the map where the pond appears as a small blue dot only serves to tease us. We have used compass, four wheel drive, and a fair amount of shoe leather.

In the end, we find the pond. We see it through the underside of spruce boughs as we descend a thickly wooded hillside. The pond reflects the sky above, and it seems like sky level has come down to sea level. The blue water, the sky water shows between the straight black spruce and cedar trunks as we walk toward it. It is six hours since we started, and we were never more than three miles from it the whole time.

In minutes, we land the biggest brook trout of our lives, a brilliant speckled native male with the characteristic curve toward the tip of the jaw. It is a fish that is one-third as wide at the girth, top to bottom, as it is long.

He is as much a part of that beaver pond as the drowned and tangled web of cedars at its edge. As much as the red and yellow October forests of the mountain in the distance. As much as the big tawny beaver who slapped his tail like a thunderclap when I scouted the shore.

That night, we ate the trout and found the pond within.

Sighting By Eye

Connectedness

Something to Write Home About

Packed jetliners coming and going. The press of crowded Caribbean tourist shops. Money draining out through credit cards. Sun, sand, and the gentle lullaby of the cruise ship. Modest sunburns. A blitzkrieg retreat from five months of shivering New England bleakness.

Instead of fresh flowers, we get fresh snow when we return.

It would be fairly typical, except for Bus A-5 in San Juan, Puerto Rico.

Plenty of time until the flight home. Cab fare to the airport is eight dollars per person. City bus fare is 25 cents each. The frugal traveler does a quick calculation and sees a chance to take home an unbroken twenty dollar bill. What have we got to lose?

Oh the humanity of it. And that's just the point.

Once on board, we learn that we must change buses out at some unknown-to-us point to catch another bus that will actually take us into the airport. The bus driver, a giant muscular man with a shaved head and dark sunglasses, assures me he will let us know when it time to get off.

As the bus fills up, including all available standing room, I begin to worry. I can not even see my wife now through the press of bodies at the other end of the bus. What if the big burly driver forgets the small Yankee way in the back?

The 15-minute, sixteen-dollar, taxi drive to the airport is now by our own doing turned into a 35-minute-long bus ride with no sign of being over.

We meander, we stop every quarter mile, we gorge and disgorge our human cargo all over San Juan. I am starting to perspire.

But then I begin to notice something. Whenever an old woman gets on the bus, the driver stops and helps her on. Once aboard he finds her a seat near the front, even if it means directing a man to get up and move. But the men all seem to know what is expected of them.

Women and children first. The toughest looking hombres get up and move back without batting an eye.

29

Sighting By Eye

Gradually, I see the bus in a new light. Instead of a mass of strangers full of the rancor of impersonality, it seems more like a family.

The guy next to me, sensing my predicament and questioning me about it, starts counting down the stops with me. As the crowd thins, a lady sitting up near my wife leans into the aisle and holds up two fingers and shouts, "Two more stops!" I would have turned around to see if she was talking to someone behind me, but I was sitting against the back of the bus.

After not seeing his face in the rear view mirror for 20 minutes, the crowd clears away and there is the shaved head of the driver and his dark glasses—looking up at me? As if to confirm this, he gives an exaggerated nod of his shiny head to reestablish contact.

I can see my wife now also, she is sitting among the almost exclusive female population in front, having an animated conversation with a middle-aged woman.

Finally it's our stop.

Ironic, but the warmest part of our Caribbean vacation was not at the beach or on the verandah deck overlooking the pool. It was on a city bus in San Juan in the company of strangers.

Maybe What Littering Is All About

A while ago I was passing an intersection on a deserted country road. A car sat at the stop sign, door open, and a young woman appearing to be in her twenties was leaning out on the driver's side. It looked as if she had poured something onto the pavement.

As I passed I noticed she was still holding something outside the car, and she turned and crouched low in the seat eyeing me intently as I passed. Something seemed odd, and I slowed down even more and then pulled over a little ways up the road. I sat watching, wondering what the person would do next.

For what must have been less than a minute, but seemed longer, there was a kind of Mexican standoff. Since this situation was near my home I intended to determine what was going on. At the same time the occupant of the car seemed unwilling to leave the spot.

Then suddenly she slammed the door shut and raced out of the intersection and past me. I made an attempt to get the license plate number but somehow missed it.

Immediately I backed to where her car was positioned to investigate. What I saw made me angry, but more I was saddened and disappointed.

There in the middle of the road at the deserted stop sign on that beautiful country road was a filthy mess. There was an enormous pile of cigarette butts, and for good measure next to it lay a large super-size paper cup along with its stale contents poured all over the place.

Once near the nature sanctuary in Mystic I approached a car which then sped off in a hurry. Slowing down I saw he had dumped a large garbage bag of trash along the grassy roadside.

Last week in Newport, while we were walking along the waterfront, we noticed two teenagers, one of whom discarded a plastic cup in the middle of the sidewalk. Moments later, when we caught up with them, I turned to the offender and told him he had dropped his garbage up the sidewalk. He just

31

stared at me showing neither surprise or shame, just a blank look.

More than just sloppy, I see these people as individuals who are missing something. They are missing awareness, conscience, and knowledge. I can't help thinking they have missed a lesson somewhere along the line, or that they have not yet matured in some way, that their growth has been stunted and choked off. And all this leaves me with a new uneasy feeling.

After time passed and I reflected on the cigarette-butt girl incident I realized that discarding garbage is a matter of degree. In a consumer society we all discard things; the cigarette-butt girl is just a more flagrant offender with perhaps uglier and less expensive garbage. Unless we buy things that rot and quickly return to their natural state, then we all contribute to fouling the planet. Sure, if we put our junk in politically acceptable places—landfills, recycling centers, and so on—we feel better and the stuff doesn't get seen so soon, but it is still with us as waste somewhere.

In his Pulitzer Prize-winning work *Turtle Island*, poet Gary Snyder tells the story of a monk and an old master walking in the mountains. They noticed a little hut upstream. The monk said, "A wise hermit must live there"— the master said, "That's no wise hermit, you see that lettuce leaf floating down the stream, he's a Waster." Just then an old man came running down the hill with his beard flying and caught the floating lettuce leaf.

Next time I start my big diesel truck and watch the sooty smoke waft into the fresh morning air, I should realize not as much as I think separates me from cigarette butt-girl. Someday the girl may wake up and stop smoking, but what about the rest of us. Unfortunately something tells me most of us will probably still be preaching wilderness awareness and pursuing that lettuce leaf down a mountain stream in a two-ton SUV.

Connectedness

Separated by a Cell Phone and a Common Language

The ball and chain of the 21st-Century is a small 3-by-5-inch electronic device know as a cell phone. It brings you into range to be interrupted any time during waking hours, and for some poor souls this may extend into sleeping hours as well.

After going cold turkey and divorcing myself of cellular service three years ago, I have again taken up with the in-touch crowd. Sensing my vulnerability and that I had willingly let my guard down, my wife enrolled me in a two-year plan (sentence). The plan guarantees to garnish 400 minutes of my life per month for a minimum payment of $20. During these precious lost minutes I must hold an object about the size of a small stone up to my ear and strain to hear people, whom I cannot see, talk.

During the first week of the seduction, I carried the little phone everywhere. In my car, on my hip, even into the bathroom. The phone company would say, and have me believe, that I am now much closer in touch with my fellow humans—including friends, family, and co-workers.

The truth is, we are drifting farther apart.

We no longer must remember to say all that needs to be said when we are with each other. We now can forget everything and call each other back to hear what we missed while we were not listening to each other in the first place in person.

After that first week of using the phone I felt drained. It was as if I was part of the Borg (that fictional Star Trek Collective) that shares a common consciousness. Except I did not share their consciousness, but their unconsciousness. The whims of others could now be foisted upon me instantaneously from a great distance and without forethought or premeditation or inconvenience on their part. The phone rings and I must answer. I talk. I stop talking. Then I would await the phone's next interruption. The outcome was another increase in stress and unpredictability. I instantly needed a vacation from this new instant togetherness.

33

I was thinking about how years ago we had a camp in Maine without any phone at all. Living there for a few days gave you a wonderful feeling of isolation and peace. Deep in the Maine woods you were protected from knowing all the things back home that you could do nothing about even if informed of.

During the second week of "being connected" I started to keep that new phone at arm's length and then some. It stayed in the car most of the time. I kept it turned off, except when making a call, which I tried to do only when absolutely necessary. I wanted very much to see the cell phone as a tool—a tool to be used skillfully and sparingly. These changes have helped. I can again feel those long spells of simple calm that come when thoughts are allowed to ferment and mature in the mind without being born into confusion and misgiving through the machinations of a wireless midwife.

The high tide of the wireless wave has come and gone for me. A miracle it is not. I can not get my $20 worth of cell-phone connectedness without disconnecting myself from the phone often. The question is not, "Can you hear me now?" but, "Do I want to hear you now?"

I don't think so.

Connectedness

Getting Into the Zone and Getting Away With It

John Jerome in his book *Stonework* said that when he builds a stone wall he can think about anything he wants. When I read that in his book, I couldn't read any further. That statement was so foreign to my own experience that I could not allow myself to be complicit with any more of his notions and quietly closed the book and put it down.

I maintain when you build a stone wall, you can think of nothing, not even building a stone wall. One old stonemason I met described this as being in the "zone." At the time it seemed odd, this crusty old man in overalls and a T-shirt espousing such a zen-like conundrum.

The truth is I had felt something like what he was talking about for years, but I wouldn't own up to it. It's not something you can talk to just anyone about, especially with your construction buddies.

"Hey man, how you doing? Did you get in the zone today?"

Yeah, right. That would get a few strange looks around the beer cooler.

And, for the record, I'd like to point out you can't find the zone, it finds you. No thought penetrates it, no mental chatter belongs to it. All time is lost, all focus is on the moment. Present yourself ready to work and learn. Woody Allen said that "90 percent of success is just showing up." I think it might be closer to 99 percent.

Technique is handy, awareness is indispensable. Learn what techniques you can, but

35

Sighting By Eye

do not overdo it, worrying about all sorts of rules and maneuvers. Keep a small handful of them ready and mastered, like a few familiar friends you feel comfortable with. Employ them and watch what happens. Scary stuff in the hands of a neophyte, indeed.

Every spring for the last four or five years I've agonized about how to give a class in stonework to adults. Usually I approach it studiously, thinking through the techniques that one must "master" in order to put a few stones together with some kind of fruitful outcome.

But this spring it occurred to me that that is not how I learned stonework myself. And that is the frightening part. I learned it quite by accident. I sort of discovered it as if it already existed within me. Can I teach that? Will my students make up their minds in the first few minutes of the class like I made up my mind about Jerome's book and drop me like a hot potato too.

I could start off in a conventional manner and then sneak up on them by working the weird stuff in. I have a fantasy that I will bring in these four beach stones I have that fit together, one on top of the other in a kind of pyramid, big at the bottom, small at the top. They balance precariously and fall down easily, from the outdoor deck railing where I keep them—when anybody more than tiptoes by—but I like to put them back together again. They are a kind of impermanent stone sculpture. But for the few moments it takes to put them together each time after they come crashing down, well, those few moments are like a glimpse into the moments of being in the zone and building a stone wall.

The question is not should I do it, but can I get away with it. I know that if I want my students to really feel the pull of doing some good work with their hands, to feel that pull strong enough so that they want to come back to it on their own long after the class is over, then I have to make sure they get a sense of what it could be like. I can't do that by teaching fundamentals only and making sure they "get their money's worth."

If I didn't know better, I'd say it seems like you can think about anything you want while teaching a class on stonework, except stonework.

Connectedness

Primitive Cultures Would Know What This Rain Meant

In more primitive cultures they would know what all this rain meant and they would know what to do about it. In our state, we must simply stand and be soaked. Or try to hide from it.

While we long for the blessed rays of sunshine to bathe our winter-worn psyches, our Doppler radar shows us where it is, our Weather Channel tells us it's coming, but in our age of enlightenment, no one can do anything about it but talk about it.

As for myself, so many days of rain put me back upon myself to ponder.

Twelve American soldiers died in Iraq last week and I know such things do not bring rain.

Years ago I stood in church during a funeral for my wife's youngest aunt and during the ceremony a gray sky opened and it poured and poured rain. You could hear it pounding on the church roof, and we felt like the heavens were crying with us. We were guilty of simple personification. But the rain felt right.

Complaining to an Irishman the other day about all the rain, I sputtered, "Why, there is so much rain it's like … like … "

"Ireland," he said in a heavy brogue. He spoke like he'd been there, knew what he was talking about.

And standing as we were on a bluff at ocean's edge in Noank, with Ireland the next stop to the northeast, I could image the tectonic plates drifting over eons. Perhaps Ireland once was a short stroll where it joined to us at the very end of Chesbro Avenue. And isn't it the Irish who have brought us many seers and sages to interpret what they have had their share of: hard times, guilt, plenty of rain, scudding leaden skies and the like.

I haven't planted my garden yet. I dragged out my stubborn rickety rototiller but it would not start and then it sat idly in the dirt covered by a tarp while more rain fell in the ensuing days. I hauled it back in the shed fearing the rain would worsen its touchy electronics. Then more rain fell.

37

Sighting By Eye

And yesterday a lady told me you need more than rain to grow things; then she pulled her hood over her aging head and went outside. Her demeanor was too sullen for such a wiry old scrapper.

We are bathed in war these days and few talk about it. It is a subtext that we ignore, though it soaks through us. But what do we expect ourselves to do. Our leaders have things in hand and they are marching forward achieving objectives, implementing plans, expecting to plant the seeds of our constitution in faraway deserts. With all this rain, I can't plant beans in my backyard.

I asked the Irishman with the heavy brogue who had traveled the world where he had felt the most uncomfortable. After a short pause he made me uncomfortable with his answer. "Here," he said.

One of America's greatest nature writers and conservationists Sigurd Olson, in his essay "Beyond The Ranges," wrote the following:

"Buck Sletton once told me something when heading out into a driving rain.
'Remember, young fellow,' he said, with the old twinkle in his eyes, 'remember, no matter how cold and wet you are, you're always warm and dry.'"

I suppose he meant, inside his soul. If you have no doubts.

Discovery

Sighting By Eye

Discovery

Mastering the Universe on the Rolling Pequot Hills

After years of ignoring one of my great shortcomings I am back at trying to master a round of golf. I like to deceive myself by saying I played my best golf at age sixteen—shooting a 44 on the back nine on the rolling hills of Pequot Country Club.

But a lot of water has passed under the bridge since then. I am not the same teenage golfer, and I am having a lot of trouble stepping in the same river twice.

While struggling with my ups and downs I also struggle to find solace and the deeper meanings and perhaps even an inkling of golf's "inner" game, which I'm sure must be contained like some heartwood inside my flailing conundrums on the course.

What is the sound of one golf ball going errant into the forest? Often it is a loud and firm "whap" when it strikes a tree. What is the meaning of a ball disappearing in deep green rough just in front of the 18th green so that no matter how long you look you can not find it? Why do some putts roll off into eternity on some greens and others stop short like a mule on a mountain precipice?

Slowly but surely I am being pulled back toward this game of my youth. Memories come flooding back with great familiarity, but the clubs still feel like foreign objects in my hands and behave in unpredictable ways as if they are possessed by some strange and unseen power.

On one hole my swing at the ball may make it go off wildly to the right. On another, the ball may hug the ground as if magnetized to the earth and not become airborne more than a few inches. On other shots my club twists in my hands like a dowsing rod finding a raging river under the fairway, causing the ball to erupt off the heel of the club and disappear forever into the nearest bushes.

But rather than even consider taking lessons, no more than I would consider taking lessons in swinging a stone hammer, which I occasionally do for

41

Sighting By Eye

a living between rounds of golf now, I am a firm believer in the holistic approach to golf.

Which reminds me: Yesterday I went to a place called Golfers Warehouse, a kind of Home Depot for golfers. Instead of a place to buy everything imaginable for would-be home repairers, this place sells everything possible to help the score-challenged golfer forget the numbers on their scorecard and become more involved with the numbers on their credit card.

Sure enough, at the back of the store, a very self-assured and fit man in a black golfing shirt handed out advice and new demonstrator clubs to anyone who asked. There's a big net and you hit them right there in the store so you can fall in love on the spot with clubs with names like Big Bertha and Killer Bee.

It's a long story, but I have been using my wife's driver off and on after trying it on the course one day and finding out that it performed better than my old Number 1 wood, which is actually made of wood—at least the head of the club is. Yes, with her titanium-headed club with light flexible shaft the ball does go farther and straighter for me.

So the man at the Golfers Warehouse kept handing me driver after driver (the club you use to tee off with) and each one felt big and clunky and unwieldy in my hands as I smacked ball after ball against the green net. Finally, hearing the story about my wife's club, he suggested I try a woman's club. I brushed him off with "no thank you," not willing to buy a woman's club just because it felt more comfortable and I could hit the ball better with it. I told him I had to "rethink the whole thing" and walked off to look for other items to buy that would improve my game.

He walked past me later in the store and tapped my arm as he passed. "Hey," he said in a deep macho golfer's voice, "don't worry about using a woman's club. I'd hit the ball with a fishing pole if it would go farther."

I dropped the whole idea of buying a new driver and bought an expensive pair of golf shoes instead. Now at least I look like I can play better.

Discovery

A Fundamental Entity of Nature Gone Wild

My electrical friend, John of Mystic, is always shocking me with how easy it is to become dead through electrocution.

Recent electrical developments have rekindled my curiosity and nervousness in regard to this subject.

John told me the other day, in one of our typical parking lot interviews, that if I have a worn spot in the rubber sole of my shoe I could provide a ground for electricity which would probably complete a circuit and result in my death. I find it unfathomable to understand how the electricity near the tip of my outstretched finger will know it has an exit point through the sole of my shoe, but my lack of comprehension will not in the least bit stop it from happening. I do not know if I have described these invisible dangers accurately, but I do know what you do not know can kill you. And John puts the fear of electricity in me.

Most people, it seems to me, are cavalier about electricity, self-assured and comfortable with it, almost careless with its lethal consequences. They use it every day, all day, and in a multitude of ways. But really, they don't know the slightest thing about it. How is it generated? How does it work? What causes it?

43

Sighting By Eye

John, who knows a great deal about it, speaks about it as if he were navigating a labyrinth of subjectivity in which the truth may or may not be known at any particular instant in a universe full of flux. Which incidentally pretty much describes reality as it is.

John knows the head count of area electrical casualties; he follows such things as if tracing a wire back to its connection. One man in a ditch with a water pump running. Extension cord run over by heavy machinery. Insulation gone. Another tries to save him. Two dead. A lineman on a pole, someone running an incorrectly installed generator in a nearby business. Severe burns. A barefoot child touches an ungrounded battery charger in a workshop and succumbs. Only 32 volts entered her body. It is amazing how little electricity it takes to kill. Expect the unexpected.

And now that electricity is in the news because of a big blackout I can see we have become totally dependent on this "fundamental entity of nature" as Webster's dictionary describes it. We live in a veritable house of cards of interlocking dependency. If the fail-safes, which are not fail-safe, fail, we are left in the dark, literally. Our water supply is unreachable, our food supply spoils, our currency stays locked away, our social fabric starts crumbling, hysteria and heat stroke fell us; all we can do is rush down to the store in snarled traffic while the gas in our tanks holds out and buy the last few batteries and bottles of water off the shelves.

My answer to this dilemma? I have none. We have not completely harnessed this thing called electricity. It is a work in progress. We cling to the planet at the pleasure of the elements and with whatever wits we have about us. We are a long way from bringing nature under control.

And if you doubt this, take note of the saddening news that in New York two people died during the blackout, killed by fire from candles used against the darkness in their homes. Even the oldest of our technologies employed by the unwary or unskilled or unlucky can prove fatal.

Soon things will be back to normal and we will forget our run-in with the dark side. The mystery of the electron-proton attraction and what those potent little nuggets of energy do to get at each other to be satisfied will be forgotten. A few heads will roll, a few wires will be replaced, and the power will continue to flow. Perhaps a windmill jouster will put up a windmill on a small efficient self-contained power grid in the countryside somewhere, but that will be it.

John, my electrical friend, will offer up some cogent advice and shake his head. And we will look back at the Blackout of 2003 and say it can never happen again. Not even expecting the expected.

44

Discovery

Fishing is More Scientific Than Ever

Having gotten away from flatfishing for decades, I never dreamed the road back would be so hard.

The first thing I discovered is that they don't call them flatfish anymore. After a careful skimming of my *Connecticut Angler's Guide*, I found something called a winter flounder, which appears to be the correct creature.

The guide's definition says, "winter flounder: A right sided flatfish with small mouth and no teeth." Close enough I decided, after studying the accompanying drawing. It goes on to say the fish "occurs in tidal estuaries, coves, and rivers over the mud and sandy bottom throughout the year." It sounds odd that it "occurs;" "lives" seems a more comfortable existence for the poor fish.

Anyway, I believe I have the right fish.

The next step will be to catch one. I can only hope that they still frequent the same haunts that they did in the 1960s and bite on the same bait.

My greatest fear is that I will set up at one of the old locations only to have a real angler—we used to call them fishermen—ridicule my lack of common sense.

A further reading of my angler's guide only adds to my misgivings. Emblazoned across the top of one section of the booklet are the words: ARE THE FISH I CATCH SAFE TO EAT? The accompanying table lists a variety of chemical additives that "occur" in fish these days.

On the list are PCBs, mercury, and chlordane.

Sighting By Eye

Most freshwater fish are recommended to be eaten only once per month. Depending on the body of water involved, many are not recommended to be eaten at all. Trout is an exception, in most bodies of water. The table allows that they can be eaten morning, noon, and night. (However check your local listings to be sure).

Flatfish, or winter flounder, is not mentioned at all. No news, I suppose, is good news.

But then I think of those muddy sediments in the Mystic River where I intend to find these flat little fellows, and I wonder, will I be able to pull them loose from the PCBs? Maybe there aren't any PCBs there? But now PCBs seem to be everywhere, where they used to be nowhere.

I also read that one of the recommended chumming methods for flats is tossing in quantities of cat food as a "strong attactor." Considering what is probably in cat food, perhaps I will end up giving Mad Cow disease to the next winter flounder I catch. The good news is that I probably will eat him before he comes down with symptoms.

I've learned that fishing hasn't changed much. It's still quite a science.

Discovery

In Search of a Body of Water Somewhere Near

You have to search a little to find this river. It is not like the Mystic River whose every glimpse is savored like sweet eye candy, prized for its ability to send real estate prices through the roof. No, this river is looked over, not upon. It is a river we have learned to turn our back on. Upstream at American Wharf in Norwich and downstream at the State Pier in New London attention is paid, but in many places in between the Thames River is neglected, a casualty to the hustle and bustle.

I first became aware of it as a child in the fifties when our big car paused at the toll booth on the Gold Star Bridge and you could peer over the then short metal railing to the water below. I remember stories of men being killed building that bridge, poured into the concrete. We all know that progress means forgetting an impediment like a river, once you see it that way and defeat it soundly.

My river guide and I launch the canoe down an embankment, over the train tracks, and out under the Mohegan-Pequot Bridge. Automobile traffic zooms by overhead. Pilings from old wharves jut out from the shore like rows of rotten black teeth. The wind on the water buffets our backs, but we trim the boat and make steady progress, he in the bow, I in the stern.

Except for the aged piers that showed we once needed the water there, every contemporary fixture, except Wilson's Marina to the south in the distance, now shows the water is merely an obstacle. Not much leads to the water; most everything leads away from it. My guide keeps up a running dialogue about history and spirit of place along the water. He tells of a trading post located nearby, about Indian battles at East Great Plains a few miles to the north, and how along the river here European and the Native American cultures collided.

We land for a respite on a dirty shore scattered with refuse: cans, paper, old tires, and rusty metal. Another set of train tracks is laid along this side of the river too, and curves along the water like a fence to keep the river out.

47

Sighting By Eye

Chatting, we stretch our legs and take a short walk up a worn-out road to the summit.

Spread before us is a wasteland. Like the river below, the former Norwich State Hospital has been deserted. Brush and weeds grow where manicured lawns once flourished. Twisting vines claw through crumbling mortar walls. A sense of emptiness and isolation permeates the place. My guide tells me the site was founded on a noble idea to help the mentally ill, but like many lofty goals fell low. It became one of the country's top lobotomy destinations. Now they plan something else for the site, with some other utopian purpose in mind—entertainment, I hear.

Suddenly, security guards sweep down on us. They shoo us back to the river like we were flotsam and jetsam and follow us right down to the water's edge to watch as we paddle away. It is as if anything conveyed on the water is trouble and they must be sure we stay off their property, which the people of Connecticut own.

So repelled, we paddle back, this time against the wind, along wide reaches of open water and small white-capped waves. The river appears more brooding and cold now, but feels alive under our slender boat and we feel alive fighting our way across.

Coming by ferry into the mouth of the river this summer, I saw only a flat slate gray expanse between two islands of commerce—Groton and New London. Without realizing, I too perceived the Thames River as something invisible, unfelt.

As the naturalist John Burroughs said, "You must have the bird in your heart before you can find it in the bush."

Discovery

The Wisdom of Chickens and Their Shepherds

I rushed outside to the sound of frantic screams. The dog was in my son's arms and the chicken was in our dog's jaws. All three looked up at me to see what I would do next.

Without missing a beat I pinched the back of the dog's mouth hard and he dropped the bird amidst a cloud of feathers.

It has been a hiatus of 40 years since I last had bantam chickens. But since the lads wanted them and I thought I wouldn't mind the eggs, we bought nine assorted creatures at $2.50 apiece from a wiry old gentleman named Mr. Duff.

Within two days the number was down to eight. Two of them had instantly taken to overnighting, roosting as it's called, in a squat pine tree next to the pen. Something got one of them, so we quickly moved the whole entourage to a covered and hopefully impenetrable pen constructed to keep them safe.

I am of the opinion that there is a correct animal out there for all of us to care for. Some animals take considerable attention; others take almost none. Chickens are somewhere near the middle, perhaps leaning slightly toward the relatively low-maintenance side of the scale.

So, depending on the person, you are best to be matched up with a domesticated beast which demands what you have to offer in the way of temperament and commitment. I find that what was right for me in 1962 is still right today. I am a confirmed chicken-man it seems. I don't feel too bad though, because as I recall, one of my favorite writers, E. B. White, was of a similar ilk.

When our dog, a Jack Russell terrier, escaped my young son's grasp he was not wearing his invisible fence collar (the collar is visible, the fence is not), so he ran unobstructed to the chicken coop and grabbed the most convenient member of the feathered family of eight. Someone hearing of the mishap sounded ho-hum. "Oh, it's in the dog's genes," they said. "And in the chicken's to be eaten?" I might add in a sarcastic manner.

49

Sighting By Eye

Somehow the boy caught the dog, who refused to give up the chicken—at that point.

The boy was exercising the dog probably because I am not a terrier man. I do not have the temperament to keep up with an animal that chases and barks at everything that moves.

If you consider all animals that humans can care for and husband, you will find a rich assortment. Now, if you consider all the possible persons suited to each breed, then it really becomes interesting. Take a man or woman who works at a fish hatchery. What might their personality be like as opposed to one who tends a herd Holsteins or a flock of sheep? The possibilities are fascinating

After I picked up the still breathing chicken and placed her with her seven siblings, I noticed that they all stayed close to her. The leader of the small flock, a fledgling rooster, even seemed to lean up against her for moral support.

Within a day she was eating and drinking again. Within two days she was venturing out into the yard again with the other seven. When all you can do is run a little and flap your wings to keep from becoming dinner and you're back on the front lines when you still have a limp from a terrier's tooth—that's what I call brave.

That's what I like about our chickens, they are afraid of everything—except bugs and chicken feed—but they still march out of the chicken coop every morning and get the job done.

If, as Woody Allen once said, "90 percent of success is just showing up," then my chickens already have the edge they need.

Discovery

Building a Tree house for the Child Inside

I'm not sure why tree houses aren't more in vogue. Why aren't a cacophony of hammers resounding through the suburban woods?

Perhaps the art of building has become too institutionalized. Too hemmed in by convention and practicality.

A friend of mine has a boatyard where unfulfilled tree-house dreams seem to be finding unbridled vent. Standing back and marveling at his latest construction project, I can see the urge for building skyward is strong. The carpenter's concoction of boards reaches upward there without much apology or logic. It's fantastic.

Too few adults build for the child inside. They build for the children they have externally, and then not often enough. I've been waiting for about two years for my tree house to be built. The promises keep coming, but so did the excuses. My kids have given up on it, I'm sure. Now that I've got the contractor in question, yours truly, to get on with the process, they don't seem to know what to think. They walk around it and look up and then go off to their more tangible and grounded sandbox. What is dad up to now, eight feet in the air?

The floor joists go on next. Construction schemes are starting to dance through my head. I am not a wood builder, never have been, but this doesn't feel like wood. It feels like a tree. Strange contradiction. Two hearty oaks stand ready to receive whatever boards I hand up to them and hang onto them.

I am dreaming about trap doors and old cast-off windows. How about a few lengths of chimney pipe and a pint-size pot-belly stove for heat in late fall and winter? Aren't there some clapboards left over from the house? Some green wood stain somewhere, and some tin for the roof? Just think what rain would sound like on a tin roof with a tiny fire crackling inside. Snow flakes drifting by would ratchet up the word "snug" exponentially and be icing on the cake.

I've never thought flying was too natural, but getting off the ground and

51

Sighting By Eye

into the trees seems to suit the psyche. Somewhere, treading water in the gene pool of our pasts, tree-living has been firmly planted. I just haven't had or made the time to explore those particular roots until now.

The only—up in the air—question is, if I build it, will my kids come.

Discovery

Looking for Water in all the Wrong Places

First we dug in the front yard. Five feet and the machine hit solid ledge.

Down in back we went six feet in one hole and then seven in another before we struck rock. I lobbied for one more attempt. This time the excavator got ten and a half feet before that vicious grating, scraping, gnashing sound signaled the end of the line.

In three days there was almost a foot of water in the hole, and in four days more it is gone.

Then I remember an old dowser that lives up the road a few miles. I call him and he doesn't get back to me. So I call him again. He finally agrees to come out with his dowsing rod.

His methodology is not what I expect. He shows up in a tiny VW pickup with a dowsing rod and a pair of brush clippers in the back, his wife in the front. She stays in the truck.

He grabs the rod and strides off into the woods to dowse. Immediately he breaks the rod he came with and sets about cutting another from a nearby sapling. I ask if the variety of wood matters. He says no, almost any kind of wood will do.

This is not what I expect. I expect some element of mystery attending the search. I expect hocus-pocus. Mumbo-jumbo. Witchcraft. Some even call this process "witching for water." Instead I get the fanfare of a man looking for a lost sock.

"How did you learn this," I ask, following him around as he paces to and

53

Sighting By Eye

fro with the rod poised in front of him. I know he has been a practitioner for many years.

"I watched a guy doing it and asked if I could try," he tells me, and he takes another step. "I tried it and it worked," he says.

He has just rediscovered a vein of water he found farther down the hill and he stops.

"You try it," he says and hands me the stick. He shows me how to hold it close, wrists and arms tucked in at your side, palms up.

I walk over the same spot expecting the stick, which is the shape of a "Y," to plunge down toward the earth, twisting and bucking in my hands.

Nothing. The great underworld of water does not beckon.

He takes the stick back and continues to work.

He walks up and down and then back and forth. He finds two veins of water that cross. He walks up to the spot again. The stick teeters and then pulls downward. He stands still at the spot. "Fifteen feet," he says. "The water is about 15 feet below the surface."

When I tell him, the excavator operator laughs out loud.

"One more hole," I ask. There is silence while he is thinking.

He shakes his head, grins and agrees to dig one more hole. This time the ledge is a little deeper and we get eleven and a half feet before the machine can't go deeper.

After a few days and a little rain, water is in this hole too. More rain, more time goes by. I am waiting it out. After two weeks the first hole is soft mud and the hole the dowser picked still holds about five inches of water. But then by his own calculation the intersecting water veins are another three and a half feet down under the ledge. We haven't got deep enough and are not likely to without more expense. This would involve dynamite. The question is, where exactly to make the commitment to drill and blast.

Despite all efforts, the truth still eludes.

The dowser left behind his stick. I take it out from time to time and turn it over in my hands. I feel like some primitive aborigine who has just been introduced to some modern wonder and is turning it over and over wondering in awe how it works.

I put the stick back and go again and look into the hole. Neanderthals were similarly stumped I'm sure.

There are no guarantees.

I buy George Applegate's book titled *The Complete Guide to Dowsing*.

I hope to find in the book what I can't find in the ground.

What I'd hoped was a question of knowing and certainty keeps turning into a question of believing.

Even George Applegate can't explain exactly how it works. But he says anyone willing to try hard and have faith can find water. You just have to link up

Discovery

with the "Universal Mind" through your subconscious and cultivate your "dowsing consciousness" in the process. I skipped a few steps but you get the idea.

It seems there is mystery everywhere and water only where you find it.

Sighting By Eye

Discovery

The World Through the Outhouse Door

Some say that all progress is advancement. I think there is a bit of irony and nuance mixed in there somewhere. My research has come from a very unusual think tank.

During the month of October I spent a lot of time out in the outhouse. Not that I was afflicted by some intestinal dismay, but rather that I have been involved in the "hole-scale" restoration, of extremely robust proportion, of an antique "four-holer" outhouse in a Noank backyard.

You know the drill: you keep most or as much of the existing material and structure as possible and permitted, while you re-construct the building into a serviceable garden shed. The landscape is not disturbed; the quaintness and historical dimension of the neighborhood is sustained. And the owner is left with both a pleasant reminder of a bygone day and more storage space.

But being in the outhouse so much, it is easy to gather a little insight into the vast strides we have taken between the 19th and the 21st century in America. The idea comes to me that the most elegant lady and the most dignified gentleman alike, had to walk or run, rain or shine, winter and summer, in full view of the rest of the neighborhood to a little wooden building at the farthest reach of their backyard to do their business. Talk about dirty laundry. But that's right, we don't hang out our laundry on the clotheslines anymore either—to dry in the fresh breezes and afternoon sunshine. But of course the breeze isn't always fresh and the sun isn't always shining. Come to think of it, the electric clothes dryer is a handy invention.

Foolishly at first, I let a little bit of nostalgia creep into my musings of the outhouse era. It seemed grand, this little building with fine copper flashing, cedar shingles, distinctive white pine siding and trim. The paint was almost gone from the ancient exterior, but the remnant swatches of cobalt blue and lively green that clung to the old wood seemed charming. I even recalled a Block Island outhouse with a graceful crescent moon and stars cut in the siding at the peak near the roof: a kind of whimsical ventilation system.

57

Sighting By Eye

Then by chance last weekend I happened to visit a modern blue plastic porta-potty at an outdoor public event. Suddenly all romance was gone. In an instant I was very thankful I had been born in the time of indoor plumbing. No matter how you dressed it up, the technology was primitive and stinky.

So as I adjourned to the workshop to repair the eight-foot-long, one-piece, pine toilet seat containing the four holes that would now become a cover for a storage compartment, I counted my blessings.

Yet I still have a tinge of doubt. Most modern changes spell improvement, but often good things are lost in the process. Sometimes replacement technologies have their own ugly side, worse than what preceded them, only it takes time to find that out. The horse and buggy was slow and the horses left reminders of their presence everywhere, but what about the tons of greenhouse gases produced by the average modern automobile every year. And what is more invasive, growing oats and hay or drilling for oil and refining it into gasoline? Horses made a mess, but nothing on a global scale that was irreversible. Breathing their fumes did not rot your lungs, just puckered your nose. And if automobiles were the work of terrorists, I doubt the astounding 40,000 killed every year by them in America would go so unnoticed.

I can't think of a similar downside to indoor plumbing except perhaps using two to five gallons of water every time you flush, or maybe all that percolation into the groundwater of so many diluted fluids and solids. But in the end, as I perch on the threshold of this reinvigorated outhouse, I know there must be something redeeming knowing your imperfections were hanging out for the rest of the world to see. Perhaps it kept us a little more honest to our true natures, if not less inconvenienced.

Discovery

It's Primarily a Mental Phenomenon

Pete Swider wipes up a small but indiscreet oil drip from under his 1969 Norton Commando fastback. A security guard gets nervous at this bit of unscheduled interactiveness with the exhibit. He is assuaged when Pete tells him it is his motorcycle he's cleaning up after in one of the grandest motorcycle exhibits of the century.

But it seems like too much of a good thing. The crowd is too big for comfort at the Guggenheim in New York City, where the motorcycles are on display in all their glory, touted as art.

It is hard to get a moment alone with the bikes amongst the milling throngs on a muggy August afternoon. There are glimpses of recognition between the bodies, like glimpses of blue sky between puffy clouds. These sleek, metallic shapes not only look the part, but unleashed from these surroundings, could perform like the wind.

Here, for this curious moment, they are stone still, sculpture only.

The exhibition, called simply "The Art of the Motorcycle," has brought us to the Solomon R. Guggenheim Museum at the corner of 89th Street and 5th Avenue.

There are exactly 99 motorcycles arrayed along the spiral concourse, each on its own pedestal. They are the cream of the crop from more than a century of

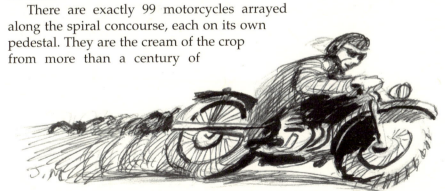

invention and inspiration and speed. Starting from 1868 and going all the way to the present, they represent the beauty and raw power of machines meant to propel the human being at inhuman speeds.

With such a historic sampling of motorcycles like this under one roof, it is easier to see the style and tone of each time and culture expressed in form and technique.

The Ducati and the Bultaco have the same suavity and curves to match. They swirl and flow like Picassos on rubber, Leonardos capped with carburetors. The BMWs are the industrial wonders, supreme engineering, impatient and eager to march on quickly and relentlessly. The British bikes have that slight romantic quality to them, like a meadow fertilized by seaweed. They have the flawed electronics, but that does not show when they stand still. I always think of a nation that is prepared to put up with the flaw and fuss, but at the same time expect the solid in temperament, when I think of the British bikes. The Japanese overcome with efficiency. And their appearance on the motorcycle scene in this America did just that. They out-produced and under-priced their competition right out of business and into museums.

Perhaps knowing what I know about the cultures that created these machines predisposes me in my opinions. But then again, when you look at them isolated in shape and form here in the museum, you do see something you hadn't before.

Here they are naked machines, with very little sheet metal to cover up their working parts. Their natures require their exposure. Air-cooled engines and other moving parts must overcome heat in order to operate. In automobiles, designers hide too much of the engineer's work. In a motorcycle it is laid bare.

On the way home, after leaving the exhibit, we are stuck in traffic on interstate 95 on the outskirts of the city, watching guys in T-shirts and sneakers selling phones, car door to car door.

It takes a good hour to clear the logjam. While we wait, the heat presses in and the cars are lined up like rows of beetles in the sun. All of a sudden there is a loud whine mixed with a screaming roar and I look up to see two motorcycles flash past in the 4-foot space between lanes of fumbling cars. Flesh and blood riding rocketing pistons, brakes, aluminum, steel, and rubber.

And Robert Pirsig, in the book *Zen and the Art of Motorcycle Maintenance*, said: "The motorcycle is primarily a mental phenomenon."

As a creation of our consciousness, the motorcycle has the capacity to move us, body and mind; there is no doubt about that.

Discovery

A Tradition of Getting Away From It All

Block Island isn't too far from the mainland, but I'm convinced it's just far enough to escape the gravitational pull of our obsessive-compulsive Swamp Yankee ethic. If my history is correct, even "a penny saved is a penny earned" and "waste not, want not" Ben Franklin came to Block Island, and I think it might have had something to do with the fair breezes and a fair young lady just over the horizon.

Folks who can't drop a tool or put down the phone in their workaday life can't hold anything but a cold drink and a few fuzzy thoughts on the "Block" as it's affectionately called. At least that's what my unscientific assessment reveals.

After years of declining invitations to accompany our relatives to the Fourth of July celebrations on Block Island, this year we went. And I'm not a bit sorry. The parade was original, the Steak Fry Dinner at the firehouse immediately following was delicious, and the crowd was fun-loving.

In the large sheltered bowl at the north end of the island known as New Harbor there were perhaps two thousand boats at anchor. At the docks, boats were rafted side by side at least six deep. Beer, ice cream, and Mudslides (a novel and powerful mixed alcoholic drink) flowed late into the night. Everywhere there were pedestrians, bicycles, and mopeds. Beached at water's edge around most of the coves were enough small inflatable boats to make you think a vast invasion force had landed, which it had.

Old hands told me the Fourth is the big holiday on the Block. Many told stories of coming out on that holiday for decades as if it were a part of an annual pilgrimage or rite of summer. Mythology is too large a word, but the stories I heard always strove to push the envelope of island memories to the limit.

Pete the retired electrician told how in the 1960s he and a friend bought a 16-foot runabout off the showroom floor, immediately launched the boat, filled up extra gas tanks, and drove straight to Block Island. The dockmaster

61

Sighting By Eye

Discovery

complained they didn't even have identification numbers on the boat. Someone on a big yacht tossed them a case of cold beer and they were set for the duration.

Another old salt used the word Tahiti in reference to the island. That perfectly sensible people would launch from the mainland, out of rivers and inlets, coves and marinas, in a kind of vacationers' Dunkirk, fleeing their workaday life of regularity and tedium for a few square miles and a few dozen hours of island bliss.

I had been to Block Island a number of times, but I had never seen it from a boat tied up at Payne's Dock in New Harbor. As a previous member of the crowd coming and going by ferry, I had definitely missed the boat. Very little occupied these self-propelled island invaders on their way to contentment. And that is the test of real relaxation and enjoyment. A simple outdoor cookout with a mini-sized gas grill became the stuff of legends, wisecracks, and sun-tanned faces. Beaming boat captains would fry up hot dogs and sausages while their families brought out the salads, pasta, and rolls. Kids lapped up ice cream cones and adults indulged in fried clams at the snack bar. They all went to the beach to alternately roast on the sand and freeze in the sea.

I recognized a workaholic guy who runs a trucking company 24-7 far inland. He had temporarily gone to seed Buddha-like behind his Foster Grants on the dock bench doing nothing but getting lost in the moment. Another man I had never seen out of his blue work clothes except for his wedding day appeared in shorts, sneakers, and a T-shirt. They say he hadn't come out to Block for the Fourth in years. Perhaps this was a sign he had turned a corner and got over his divorce.

On Fourth of July eve a crowd of us streamed out of Ballard's Restaurant and across the docks laden with boats full of revelers celebrating the nation's independence and some of their own. Ahead of the others and barely within my earshot, one island visitor cast a look around him and murmured:

"To be young again."

I'm not positive what he meant, but I think Tahiti in New England was to blame.

Rebellion

Sighting By Eye

Inside a Florida Maximum Security Unit

We shuffled into the rented minivan for what I knew would be a little drive to Daytona.

Despite the 19-hour trip ahead of us, some of the characters in the back seat were already laughing and joking and watching movies on a DVD player smuggled aboard.

I steeled myself, buckled my seatbelt, and we are off.

The intervening states were a blur. The high point topographically was probably crossing the Hudson River on the lower deck of the George Washington Bridge, which I had never done before. The view was stupendous. It was the first tunnel "above" water I have ever been in. After that it was all lowlands, or "flatlands," as my Vermont friend and truck mechanic philosopher Ron calls this part of America.

We drove and drove and arrived in the dark, just as we had left, with a minimum of fanfare. My in-laws were waiting to activate the steel-barred gate to let us in. I smiled and drove the minivan down into a ravine of concrete, security cameras, and protective barriers. I could hear the gate come down behind us and lock in place with a resounding finality.

I was quick to learn the first rule of maximum security living: you can not leave this place without a key.

The one exception was the tall iron pedestrian gate that leads from the outdoor pool area to the beach. That one has a combination lock which was easy to remember because the two digits you must dial are the same as both my current age and the year I was born. What are the chances of such a coincidence? Every morning I passed merrily out that gate for my daily exercise period, a 45-minute walk on the beach.

There are little black cameras located at all high-risk areas. They are at the entrances and exits of course, but they are also in places like the closet-like romance novel library and the treacherous billiards room. Once when I was alone in the hot tub I looked up at the lens of the omnipresent camera and

Sighting By Eye

remembered it was at least a twosome. I felt relatively safe in the sauna, but you never know. There is also a camera aimed at the mail boxes in the lobby, and every day when the mail arrives someone stands up a little white sign that reads: Mail In. You can see that sign from Channel 2 on any TV set in the building.

Standing in the plastic-flower-and circulating-waterfall-filled atrium you can look up and see the balconies of 23 floors, toward which the front doors of all the units face. There is no 13th floor for obvious reasons. It reminds me of all those prison movies where you can look up at the cellblock tiers and see the doors of all the cells facing in.

Staying on the 12th floor, at about the vertical middle of the building, I couldn't help thinking about the possibility of an earthquake. I was too far off the ground to jump off the oceanside veranda without a parachute, but not high enough up to avoid being squashed by the missing 13th floor and the next 11 floors above that if things started shaking. But who ever heard of earthquakes in Florida. It's all built over swamps and quicksand, right?

But people love it. They work all their natural lives up north and then sell everything and buy one of these super-safe condo units for about $417,000. Then the hurricanes—which may or may not be more prevalent because of all the global warming due to all their working up north—come and blow away what they've saved and sacrificed for. It's quite a natural cycle when you think about it.

The other day, after we returned from Florida, a woman outside a nearby donut shop approached me as I was getting into my car. She asked did I have "a dollar for Christmas." Thinking fast I said, "No, but I've got 50 cents," and fished it out of my pocket. She took it and ambled quickly into the alley and away from the prying eye of the authorities.

She could never have got away with that in the hot tub in Florida. A cold and sobering thought on Christmas Eve.

When Fast and Furious Meet the Old Dirt Track

The fast and the furious have come to a dirt road near me. And in a way I am one of them. I am not fast, but sadly, I am furious.

For 14 years I have walked and run on a small unpaved town road a quarter mile from my house. It was once a place of serene quiet and unblemished woodland vistas. This little ribbon of packed gravel snakes through maple, oak, and silver birch, climbing hills and turning corners in an easy meandering way. I have learned its bends and rises and can shut my eyes and see it go.

When I started putting my feet on it in 1992 there was one house on the first mile of it. Now there are eight houses and more being built.

I remember the spot on the road where my old brown Retriever stopped walking, exhausted from what I later learned was a severe heart condition. It was on the road's steepest climb, and he stood there and could go no further. I had to run all the way home and bring back the car.

When my oldest son was six we took our first long bike ride on the road. We made a big circumnavigation that loops and links with a tar road on the way back. I remember the innocent bliss of riding on the road with him without a care in the world. There was no worrying about cars, for there were very few and those usually chugged along at a snail's pace. The posted speed limit was 15 mph and most folks kept close to that.

But things have changed. With all the new houses and the apparent use of the road as a shortcut to the north part of town, cars are more numerous and they go fast.

I used to walk the road in a quiet daze, lost in my thoughts and plodding along. It was a refreshing respite after work. When the slow drone of a motor vehicle approached, there was always ample time shake off a daydream and move to the grassy shoulder. When I had the dog with me, he'd run a hundred feet ahead and I'd call him back and make him sit by my side while the car passed. I did this with my old dog and the new one too.

Sighting By Eye

In many cases when a car passed the driver and I would exchange a neighborly wave or nod. The road did not have an anonymous feel to it like most tar roads do. The road didn't seem like just a means to get somewhere, but a destination on the way.

Lately, especially in the last year or two, many drivers who pass you on the road don't wave, don't slow down, and act like the dirt road is just an impediment delaying their arrival at someplace more important.

Ill-advisedly, I admit, I have on occasion vented my frustration by motioning to some of the fastest drivers to slow down. But I have found it does not work. They are shamed and become more angry and agitated than they already are, at a life that makes them rush to and fro without relief.

One evening about dusk a car roared over a hill at about 40 mph and I had to jump to safety on the side as it drew abreast of me. I waved my arms for it to slow, but the driver sped up instead.

Recently a man stopped in an SUV and yelled at me while I calmly told him the speed limit was 15 mph. "Who do you think you are, Deputy Dawg!" he bellowed. His face was contorted with rage, watery eyes bulging. "Don't you know there's a leash law in this state," he barked. I hadn't been paying close enough attention and barely had time to get my dog out of the road. He spun his tires on the dirt when he pulled away to send a message—don't tell him what to do. His car, his road, his world. None of my business.

The shame is on me too; my face was also shaded in anger as I waved my arms to slow him down in the first place. I bear part of the blame, as interloper.

So I have let the road go. They will turn it into tar soon enough. The dog and I walk in the woods behind the house now, neither of us wants the pull of a leash. Or the absence of peace.

Rebellion

Sighting By Eye

Grass is a Habit Worth Breaking

The grass season is upon us. Another locust devouring our most valuable commodity, time.

When I was about ten years old my father caught me kneeling at my bedside praying that he wouldn't be able to fix the lawn mower. I think he blew a fuse, as they say, when I confessed the theme of my supplication.

I've never understood the common preoccupation with larger and larger sprawls of this manifestation of suburban and now even rural blight. I see grass cutting as the most useless job on the planet.

You cut it so that it is neat and wonderful and in about four days you have to do the same exact job all over again. You could say the same thing about washing the dishes I suppose, but food does seem more of a necessity.

Grass, once fit only for cows and horses, has been recycled as a sign of affluence and prestige. The siren song of the well-tuned lawn tractor has lured many, but not me.

Yes indeed, I have been cured of the grass habit. As a direct outcome of my upbringing, my house is surrounded by a wooded lot in a relatively natural state. There are a few herbs and a wild flower or two, and I once a year trim away the small sprinkling of undergrowth, but grass does not line my driveway, thank you very much. We have a tiny lawn adjacent to our front steps, about 25 by 25 feet, and another one in the back about the same size. Half the time my wife cuts it, and when I do the job, the whole project, weed whacking included—which is really grass whacking—takes about 35 minutes. About twice as long as doing the dishes.

Last year my wife wanted the lawn greener, and after much stalling and protesting, because I knew it would grow faster as a result, I agreed. Finally unleashed, she fertilized it so heavily that she killed a substantial portion of the previously not-so-green grass. It turned straw color to my well-concealed joy.

I like Henry David Thoreau's take on over-encumbrance:

Rebellion

"How many a poor immortal soul have I met well-nigh crushed and smothered under its load, creeping down the road of life, pushing before it a barn 75 feet by 40, it's Augean stables never cleansed, and 100 acres of land, tillage, mowing, pasture, and woodlot. The portionless, who struggle with no such unnecessary inherited encumbrances, find it labor enough to subdue and cultivate a few cubic feet of flesh."

I take sweet solace in watching an owner of a massive property on the oceanfront chained to his lawn mower, a slave to a weed-whacker chasing down his green renegades, while I toil at my trade of stonework—which I expect will last for a few years unattended at least, once put in its proper place.

But the story does not have a happy ending. My father having passed away some time ago, I have been cutting his lawn all these years again. This year it has been harder than most to find the time to get the job done. I suspect on some level within me, the revolt is again close to the surface. While the 10-year-old had no time away from play to spare, the 45-year-old has begun to realize the days grow shorter with every passing summer, and he had better think twice about wasting any more of them.

Sighting By Eye

Rebellion

Iwas walking east on Church Street in Mystic when the police cruiser pulled over to the side and parked facing me. At first I thought he was pausing politely to let me pass into the parking lot, where my car was parked. There I intended to eat the lunch slung hobo-style over my shoulder.

The windshield of the cruiser was a reflection of the sky and you could not see into it. But as I advanced and started to move to my left at right angles away from the car the occupant leaned toward the open passenger window and summoned me to him.

I had learned that in a free society you can not walk away from someone in authority when he commands or curls his index finger otherwise. This went back to my Army days in Texas, when once on leave and hitch-hiking from San Antonio to Killeen a state trooper in Ray-Bans made me tramp across an interstate entrance ramp with a hook of his finger so he could eye-ball my identification papers. There was flatly no choice in the matter for the law abiding citizen.

The officer today wore the same kind of sunglasses, the kind you cannot see into. He asked me, "Were you at the Whaler's Inn?"

"No, I was not," I said. I did not tell him, but I don't think I've ever been in the Whaler's Inn in the 50 or so years I have been living or working around Mystic.

"Where do you work?" he asked me.

I told him and when he asked me who for, I told him that too. But suppose I did not work? Do I look like a vagrant with my scruffy beard? Do the suspenders I wear in a world of belt-lovers mean I will be less likely to uphold the law? Is my gait a bit slippery or do I lean to far to the left or right?

He paused and continued to look at me through the sunglasses.

"Are you sure you were not at the Whaler's Inn?" he asked again. At this point in our conversation I suppose either I was being accused of having a poor memory, or lying. Or maybe the whole thing is a ploy that will make me sweat or stumble in my alibi.

75

Sighting By Eye

"No, I was not there," I repeated. He let the moment drag out and stared at me with eyes I could not see. I waited too, saying nothing, doing nothing.

After a moment he dismissed me, and I walked into the parking lot, ate my lunch, and never looked back

I gather the reason I was stopped was that an ex-president I once voted for was in town.

I can't help think that if I was dressed like a tourist or he only got a chance to see my Volvo wagon and my nice house with white lattice over the door that he would never have pulled me aside. The noonday grime and sweat on my workingman's clothes does nothing for me.

About 15 minutes before my encounter on Church Street with the officer in the cruiser, I passed a man in a dark suit on Holmes Street. When this fellow passed, his suit jacket parted and I saw the glint of a gold shield riding at his belt. I nodded a greeting. He did not show any sign of recognition or hello, but instead locked his eyes on me, slipped off point as if he'd seen right through me, and then continued to scan the street. I did not know it, but I had already been vetted well before I met sunglasses.

I do not know what the one saw in me and the other did not.

Some rebellions can't be deciphered at a glance, but run deep, beyond the grip of glances long and short to divine.

Rebellion

On the Cutting Edge of Renewable Energy

One by one my chain saws have dwindled away. The starting spring on the small one broke last winter. The big one went down with multiple systems failure this fall. Everything from the ignition switch to the carburetor stopped functioning. I gave them both away to a neighbor who has a friend who collects such wrecks.

My oldest, and now only chain saw, a banana yellow, all metal, Pro-Mac-10-10 from the late 1960s is still running and cutting, but marginally, with bent bar and raspy exhaust. It is a family heirloom of sorts, bought new by my father and passed down to me over time. If it were to die completely I would keep it anyway, enshrined in the shed for posterity, as it holds too many memories to send away to the scrap heap.

Combine this chain saw die-off with reduced oil output in Iraq, hurricanes, oil profiteers, and many other circumstances I have no idea of, and I became quite convinced I would become cold or broke this winter; perhaps both.

Since I heat my home with oil and supplement with wood, my knee-jerk response was to feverishly visit numerous hardware and small equipment stores to see if I could bolster the bottom line of a couple of Scandinavian chain saw companies. The cheapest top-of-the-line saw from one brand was $159.95, and the cheapest saw from the other was $269.95. However, most of the chain saws these companies sell, which any normal self-respecting high-end consumer would purchase, cost $300 to $400 or more.

77

Sighting By Eye

In frustration I came home and grabbed one of several antique handsaws I had collected over the years and started to saw some wood. I tried five different style saws, everything from a huge-toothed 50-year-old one-man Disston crosscut, to a 42-inch-long bow saw which my friend in Vermont gave me a decade ago. He told me as he put it in my hands, "this saw cut a lot of firewood for my grandfather." What, back in the 1960s?

They were all as dull as butter knives.

The chain saw fairy started to whisper in my ear as I broke a sweat friction-cutting a modest four-inch-thick sapling with one of my antiques. If I persisted I would probably catch the log on fire about the same time I cut through it. "Buy the new saw," the little voice said. "You deserve it. Anyway, what if a natural disaster strikes and you need to cut up a lot of trees that fall on your house, in front of your car, or in your yard?" A real man has to have a fancy new brrm-brrm chain saw at his disposal, doesn't he? For emergencies.

The Whole Earth catalogue side of me resisted. One more gas engine in the family. What if I just bought new blades for the old saw frames and cut up small, already dead trees. Wouldn't that work for the planet and me too. So off to the hardware stores, large and small I went. I noticed the chain stores stock only standard run-of-the-mill-size blades. Twenty-four-inch-long or less—they have. Try to find a 36-inch or a 42-incher at your local Mega Store, and they would laugh you out of their 20-acre parking lot.

Finally, in a tiny tucked-away surplus store that stocks everything from plastic flowers to Chinese socket wrench sets, there, in a dusty corner amid various far-eastern plastic-handled carpentry saws, I found the mother-lode of Swedish and Danish hard-toothed bow saw blades. All sizes. Sandvik and Jacks. Brand new shiny, still in the wrapper, 36-inch blades for $2.49 each, plus tax. Ever cautious, I bought just one, to see how it would work.

Fantastic. I breezed through a 6-inch log in about 25 strokes. (About 40 seconds, for the time-impaired.) Meanwhile, I have an aerobic workout fit for a king. There's some sweat involved, but the fuel is easy to come by and can be quite tasty. Anything from tangy lasagna to steaming Irish oatmeal, to a nice tall glass of chilled apple cider will keep this saw motor running.

I have resolved to return to that store and buy more saw blades. I know I am only nibbling around the edges, but a gallon of oil saved is a gallon of oil earned, to borrow from an old saw.

Rebellion

Naming Names

I walked by the boat and tried to pronounce the name but got tongue-tied enough to break my stride and stood stammering. It was there at Champlin's Marina on Block Island that I began to see the crisis in America reflected on the sterns of our boats.

I studied the name carefully and realized that the "minium" part at the end had thrown me.

I took a deep breath and let myself only whisper the word, for fear that Poseidon, the Greek god of the sea, would throw seaweed or a tidal wave my way. "Aquaminium," I murmured with a shudder. I could feel the blood drain from my face and an emptiness in the pit of my stomach.

There, stern to the dock, sat a boat that looked like a giant floating hot tub. Its occupants sat chatting gaily on large puffy white seats. They had done their best to make a floating suburbia.

As I am about to re-name an old boat, the names people give theirs has taken on special interest for me. So for the rest of my week holiday at Block Island I carried around a small notebook and made numerous jottings about the names of boats at the marinas there. My research was done mostly at

Sighting By Eye

Payne's Dock and Champlin's, but I also did a few observations out in the harbor paddling around in my tiny foldable kayak.

At one point I thought it prudent, before being swamped, to turn my bow into the stern wake of a large ostentatious fiberglass yacht heading out of the harbor. I looked up at her towering profile as she sped past and read the name "Aspen Alternative." I had to read it twice I'm sure, as it came close to wanting to be pronounced: "Aspirin Alternative." Here was yet another case where luxury land living had been commingled—at least in the mind of the owner—with what a boat was meant for. This 70-foot, a least three million dollar yacht plowing the water before me had an evil twin in Aspen and it was being announced to the world unabashedly.

High up in the light air of this Aspen though, I think there must not be much direct knowledge of the ocean, just the views and vistas of the far ranges, the big picture, as it were. In my tiny kayak I could reach out and touch salt water anytime and gather viscerally the micro-frames of experience at no extra charge. As one former Jesuit once told me, I, in my little boat, am closer to what all those on the water profess to be seeking.

At first I had thought to give my newly fixed up old boat a strong, understated name that would show everyone how strong and understated I am. But I have now scuttled that idea. I can see that the higher we aim with a name, the lower the craft creeping through the water weighted down with it becomes.

A sampling of other boat names in my survey includes: "Wild Child," "Virtual Reality," "Wave Function," "Plastic Paradise," "Flat Out," and "Knot Home."

I do question what it means to be home or not home while drifting without purpose or direction. And what does it mean to be flat out in a world steeped in similarity and conformity. I can see that there is a strong impulse to make a cute play on words that tie if possible into the cosmology of the boat's owner. The boat then becomes a Lexus for the water, a floating billboard for Mr. Big Stuff.

Compare my friend Dave, who would go to bed at 5 o'clock after work on a Friday night and get up six hours later at 11 p.m. By midnight he was passing Stonington Point in his Greenwich 24-footer heading to Block Island. He would turn off all his running lights and ghost along in the shimmering darkness watching the phosphorous trails in the water. He would lose all track of time and sail straight through the night. At dawn he would arrive in a world of light and splendor at Great Salt Pond. He says he loves those memories and is now taking them into his old age with great fondness.

I don't know what name Dave gave his boat. But I do know he used it to go places no condo alternative could tread water in.

Rebellion

The Difficulties in Coming to a Complete Stop

Teaching my son good driving habits has put me in opposition not only him, but also with a good portion of the human race. He, like many people nowadays, can not bring themselves to come to a complete stop at a stop sign.

When I push the matter from the back seat, my wife tells me to be quiet. I reply that I will not be silenced on the matter. I am ready to take a stand. I sit thinking how diametrically opposed we are on the subject. My son keeps driving. At the next stop sign he comes to a complete stop and the driver behind comes within a hair's breadth of ramming us. They never expected such behavior at a stop sign. I am temporarily silenced. Complete and total stopping is too risky.

My wife, countless wayward drivers, and now my son, do this little finesse thing that makes it look like they are making a good-faith effort, but it is a fiction, and at the last moment, just before the car comes to a comfortable rest, they release the brake pedal and the car jumps forward. There, they have "stopped" they will tell you. Not stopping is pragmatism, self-defense. I am the idealist, the back seat driver who advocates the impractical.

My contention is that the issue goes deeper than just brake-pedal shenanigans.

I believe many 21st-century drivers cannot bring themselves to come to a complete stop anywhere, at any time, on the road or off, and it is symptomatic of a larger and more pervasive condition. They must be moving, agitating, bouncing, or they are not happy.

Let's face it, everything today is touted as "non-stop." You go to the movies for non-stop action-packed entertainment; car dealers have non-stop savings in non-stop TV commercials. We are doing everything with a simple mandate: no time to stop. We eat "fast-food" "on the run." We wield the scary phrase "24-7," which means something going on twenty-four hours a day, seven days a week, and we are proud of our inability to be at rest. I don't want to do anything that uninterruptedly except maybe breath.

Sighting By Eye

Rebellion

I tell my 16-year-old son that coming to a complete stop at a stop sign is a zen thing that will put him in touch with the car during the driving experience. It brings everything together in one quiet moment; you look both ways, pause, collect yourself, and then proceed with caution. Can you think of a better way to get through the day?

He looks at me like I have just landed from another planet and rolls his eyes. His 88-year-old grandmother who happens to be riding with us in the back seat on the way to a picnic, makes a more concrete statement about how "if you get caught misbehaving on the road at your age you will lose your license and won't get it back until you're 25." If that were only true, but he knows it is an idle threat.

As an additional test I direct him to a shortcut north of Flanders Road in Mystic which he has never been on. There is a half-mile stretch of town road there with ruts and holes that demand slowing down to a crawl. He hits the first hole with a crash, the car bouncing wildly and almost bellying-out on the gravel. He is only doing about 15 miles an hour but that is about 15 times faster than required. I tell him to slow down. His grandmother chimes in again from the back seat but I cannot hear her over my warnings and admonishments.

"Why did you ever tell me to come this way," he moans. He can not bring himself to slow down sufficiently. Another row of ominous ruts beckons. Pits and holes stretch out as far as we can see like hand grenade craters. The car continues to buck and shudder perilously.

I am more relieved than he when we reach solid pavement again.

His grandmother regards us both suspiciously from the back seat.

She is probably wondering if she can get me to come to a complete stop too, sometime.

Definitely Something About Mary

Mary called into a radio talk show during the Gulf War in 1991.

As I remember, it was just prior to the ground assault and most everyone had an opinion about the impending battle.

I didn't hear the call myself, but learned about it secondhand.

When she got on the air, Mary did not talk about the war. She had called about squirrels. It was winter, and there had been a shortage of nuts or acorns, or whatever squirrels need to survive, and she was very concerned about their well-being.

Mary lives in a convalescent home now and I have only seen her once or twice in recent years. But I have not been able to forget hearing about her phone call.

Initial reaction was almost to laugh, but then after a moment, a strange uneasiness set in. A whirlwind of public discussion was raging and in the midst of that, in a very innocent and almost naïve way, she was besieging us to look into our backyards and at our nut gap.

Mary's priorities were not the priorities of the average citizen. I don't think she thought like the rest of us. Her thinking was not misguided, but simply guided by different forces. She was not hypnotized by what mesmerizes the majority.

We kept our horse on her little farm for years, and I went there every day—perhaps a thousand times to feed him. I would see Mary often, ambling though her haphazard flower beds, or among her makeshift chicken coops. She always had a good word and was usually intrigued about something she had encountered.

It was like stepping into a different world, not because her yard was so unusual, but because her interpretation of her yard was so novel. Bees and flowers and sparrows had the status of heads of state. Her two mongrel dogs, Iris and Jakie, took on human qualities, to hear her converse with them. In little fleeting glimpses, visitors started to see the world as she saw it, at least

84

Rebellion

until they turned back on the main road again, which was just at the bottom of her driveway. She had been a registered nurse and had seen people at their best and worst for 50 years, which made me believe she knew a few things that I did not.

At times of great turmoil, and in the face of vexing problems, we are looking for a sage. With the war in Kosovo, or with the killings at the high school in Colorado, we are numb-struck, yearning for answers.

Mary in her prime would have rung up the radio station and got us to stop and take a long, hard look at ourselves by looking at—oh I don't know—maybe a bouquet of flowers.

Sighting By Eye

Civilization

Sighting By Eye

Civilization

Running with the Volvo Crowd Has its Price

It is no secret that people judge you by what you drive.

In the last year I have gone from a Ford F-350 pickup to a Volvo wagon and I have had to pay the price. Not financially—the Volvo cost less—but in the psychic sense.

In this neck of the woods, few people drive cars with a purely utilitarian motive. Yes, there is an identity thing tied up in most of our cars. Now driving the Volvo I have unwittingly put myself into the European luxury car class. If my Volvo was little older and tattered, I could escape that label and be classed as a semi-conforming, utilitarian, laid back, wine-sipping, tofu eater. However, I do not make the cut with a 1994 850 non-turbo wagon. I think the vehicle comes under the heading not-too-affluent soccer mom's car.

In the luxury class that I am now a member of, I am at the bottom of the totem pole. I was recently accosted by a BMW driver who had the gall to try and wave me out of his personal passing lane. I popped the Volvo into "sport" setting (which embarrasses to say that I have such a setting in a car that I drive) and promptly vacated the lane. Driving my big red one-ton Ford diesel pickup, this would never have happened to me. The BMW guy would be shaking in his bucket seats as I roared by, the tops of my tires even with his eyeballs.

The other day when I went in to buy a trailer hitch for my Volvo, the tough guy at the truck company parts department asked me in his best "I'm trying to be benevolent "voice" if I was "mechanically inclined" enough to bolt the trailer hitch on myself. They never asked me if I was "mechanically inclined" when I ordered a remanufactured engine-oil cooler for my F-350's 7.3 diesel motor and put it on myself.

But the weirdest part is, I am starting to take on the characteristics of a Volvo person, whatever that is. Being treated like one, I have started to buy into that self-fulfilling prophesy, morphing chameleon-like into a touchy-feely cerebral. Men in big brawny pickup trucks do not let me go in front of them in a line of traffic anymore. When I tried to slip in the other day, the guy in the city-block-sized GMC acted like I didn't exist. He and his passenger wouldn't even make eye contact with me. However, people in little benign cars are starting to smile and let me go ahead of them. If they only knew where I came from. The battle lines have been drawn and I am definitely on the other side now.

At first I tried to fight it and thought if I threw a rugged phalanx of racks on the Volvo's roof at least I would get out of the soccer mom category. I did that, but with a Swedish name like Thule blaring from the roof top I have fallen in with yet another unfamiliar crowd. Those who snow-board and mountain bike and do who knows what else.

Casting about for some anchor to slow my descent into unfamiliar territory, I remembered a bumper sticker that if employed would certainly de-Volvoize my car and put the brakes on my new, uneasy persona. The sticker reads: "Earth First. Then We'll Log The Rest Of The Planets." But I couldn't do it. I do like trees and think they should be respected and not wasted like any other living thing. And I believed that when I was driving the F-350 and expect to keep right on believing it.

Volvo drivers don't have a corner on correct thinking, they just think they do. Ditto that for macho truck men. I think I can say that for a fact now that I know where they both are coming from and how they get there.

Civilization

Life With the Boring Parts Left Out

Gravedigger spun in repeated 360-degree turns spewing airborne waves of brown dirt in all directions. The spectacle was so loud and unsettling as to awaken the dead, or put the living into a state of deadness.

With my fingers jammed into my ears I could still feel the loudness of the noise vibrating through my stomach. I held a sweatshirt hood over the lower half of my face when my hands were free in a futile attempt to filter out the wicked exhaust stench that filled the Hartford Civic Center.

This all happened at a monster truck event known as "Monster Jam," which I in my naïve ways had allowed myself to be lassoed into, on a recent Saturday night. My youngest son had gone to one of these things once, but whatever he told me about it, I did not pay close enough attention. I must have nodded half-listening while clues to saving my central nervous and auditory faculties were aired. In retrospect, he did say something about getting a headache from the fumes.

The evening kicked off after a long wait in line at the door—with a frisking. It was the first relatively thorough frisking I had ever experienced. The man doing the frisking hit my car keys, which are held together by a clip ring, and for that, or some other reason, he demanded to see them. In the other pants pocket, however, he missed my LeatherMan Micro with its small leather lanyard. We were all through the checkpoint save my oldest son's friend, who when he spread out his arms and opened his coat revealed a full-size LeatherMan in a nylon sheath. The frisking crew had a field day and quickly and efficiently stripped him of his handy tool. The item would be confiscated or some member of our party would need to take it off the premises, which meant I had to walk it to our car in a distant parking lot.

The evening was mostly about loud noise and outrageous innovations in fossil fuel consumption. Eight old cars and one full-size Ford van, which

91

Sighting By Eye

looked almost repairable at the start, were squashed into pulp metal by close of business.

For my personal pleasure, and as a diversion between monster truck escapades, three fellows on souped-up dirt bikes repeatedly risked their lives jumping 40 feet through the air and momentarily letting go of their motorcycles in the process. I could only pray for their safety at such dangerous undertakings, and when the master of ceremonies challenged them and the audience to heightened folly by attempting more dangerous stunts, I was probably the only voice of reason in the crowd against the idea. I was pitifully drowned out by a roar of "Yes!" from the masses that had come to get all the stimulation their cerebral cortexes could take. In the end one fellow did jump 20 feet in the air and 40 feet out onto a landing ramp with a black hood over his helmet and survived through no fault of his own.

Another side show consisted of several races between groups of men on four-wheel contrivances known aptly as "quads." These individuals, to the crowd's delight, raced wildly around the dirt surface that had been placed over the arena floor and like their monster cousins made lots of noise and stink in the closed space.

Every once in a while, lest we forget why we had come, a few monster trucks would rumble back into the room to run over the increasingly flattened row of cars. After the grand finale the driver of the premiere monster truck, Gravedigger, climbed out of his machine and grabbed the announcer's microphone. He was a diminutive man with a high-pitched voice. It reminded me of the man behind the curtain in the *Wizard of Oz*. He said something unintelligible since my hearing could no longer register at that frequency.

It struck me like a lightning bolt that this entire exercise was just "theater." For these folks packed from floor to ceiling in the Civic Center it was their theater. And someone did say, "Theater is life with the boring parts left out." I was just surprised how much was left out.

Civilization

Maine: The Way Life Was Until You Came

The woman stood smack dab in the middle of the parking space in the middle of Ogunquit, Maine, in the middle of a wicked August traffic jam and refused to budge.

The guy in a black Saab wagon in front of us saw the empty spot and pulled up to back in. I held back and gave him plenty of room to maneuver.

At first I thought the woman just happened to be paused on the pavement in the midst of the maelstrom caught between two thoughts or two destinations. But then as the Saab backed deeper into what might have been the only empty parking spot in town, the woman held her ground. The Saab paused, then backed closer to her.

Meanwhile traffic behind me stood still on Route 1 for a quarter mile in 90-degree heat. The Saab's bumper came closer to the woman's leg and she moved a little. I blew my horn to warn her of impending collision. In the next moment it struck me that the woman didn't want to move. She was saving a parking space for someone. We didn't know whether to laugh or swear. I think we did both.

Another moment ticked by and then the Saab driver had had it with the foolishness and just backed up slow and steady in a way that the woman had to move, and she did. She abruptly turned around and walked away, but her left hand shot up with the middle finger extended toward that gorgeous blueberry sky.

It's not exactly the Maine I used to know. The billboard at the border says, "Maine: The Way Life Should Be."

There we had two humans playing chicken for a parking space and one was on foot. Crowds, high heat, and frayed vacationing nerves will do that kind of thing, especially when neither party comes from the State of Maine. Maybe that's part of the trouble with Maine these days, most of the people there aren't from Maine.

Thank goodness the locals are stoic and have a sense of humor.

Sighting By Eye

Civilization

One sign at nearby Perkins Cove said that you are now in a Crunch Zone. "If you park here, your car will be crunched."

In one of the colorful red and green "trolley" buses we met an equally colorful driver. He started off the ride by telling the passengers there was a two-hour limit to the ride. What two hours? Weren't we just going uptown? Not another vacation nightmare, I worried?

But then he started out of the parking lot singing the country and western song "On The Road Again," and telling redneck jokes about "finding cars you didn't know you had when you cut your lawn." He did this over the loud speaker while looking at us in the overhead mirror with a toothy grin.

When we hit the traffic and started to crawl along, he asked us if we wanted to hear a poem he had composed. He started in on about ten verses that dealt directly with our current predicament. It was about tourists riding his bus, and it almost made you wish you could wait longer in the traffic so you could hear more of this one-man act. Our 13-year-old son, who now thinks nothing is fun if we think so too, asked us if we could just stay on the bus and ride around.

My wife didn't want to get off at the hotel. "Let's get off on the return trip," she pleaded. But since some passengers were already standing without seats I thought that would be selfish and we got off.

All the people I met in ice cream shacks, clam shacks, lobster shacks, and shacks in general were quite nice. They did not have that numb detachment that you find in many such jobs elsewhere, they treated us in a friendly, outgoing way, like they were actually thinking about what they were doing when they were waiting on us. I was the one who had to snap out of it and act human when they asked, "How are you today?"

Now, home safe and recovering from our holiday in Maine, something an old Mainer said a generation ago haunts me. After hearing an enthusiastic visitor compliment him on such a beautiful State, he replied dryly, "It won't be if more like you come."

Sighting By Eye

Civilization

Digging into Our Gardening Roots

Despite the supermarket's seductive call, there are still a few backyard vegetable gardeners who grow to eat. Like burning wood for heat though, you can find easier ways to stay warm, and in the case of gardening, easier ways to stay fed.

This year is a good example. Late and harried, I planted my meager vegetable garden today. I watched myself lay down the seeds in haste, aware that I was rushing what should otherwise be a hallowed experience.

Something has compelled me to have a garden in recent years, especially since I have my own land in which to plant it. And I think I finally know why.

Decades ago, a distinguished and learned man described my father as "close to the soil." At the time I found this assessment odd and faintly amusing. I thought the man was too imbued in book learning and academics to know what land and dirt had to do with us. To me my father seemed not so much committed to the soil as just unable to detach himself from it. He worked at a construction trade but continued unabated, year after year, with his cumbersome little farm and demanding rows of vegetables. I do remember his ability to grow, in particular, cabbage and onions was unparalleled in the neighborhood.

I learned techniques haphazardly from him, but never harvested the finer points he might have possessed. It was a drudgery to me that I did not care to excel at.

It did not occur to me until recently that I am possibly at the end of a previously unbroken chain of garden-makers that goes back thousands of years. I view this not so much with pride as with curiosity.

The pedigree that I inherit seems indisputable, however. The idea that my father's family in eastern Europe—going back to the Dark Ages and beyond—could ever afford not to grow what it could in the soil is nonsensical. Not to have a garden would be virtually a suicide sentence, given nourishment was so scarce there, even down to my father's generation. You would be dead

97

Sighting By Eye

in a month or two if you had to depend upon what you could afford as a peasant living in a dirt-floored hovel.

Even in my father's case, despite best efforts, he as a child in Poland suffered from malnutrition so harsh that he went blind for a time. He was treated by the village medicine woman, who squeezed a yellowish paste out of a wild plant and spread it over his eyeball with her tongue. He regained his sight, but the scaring of his eyes was so profound that doctors would marvel that he could see at all.

I still know a few old timers that have a vegetable garden, but even most of them have let the thing lapse to hay field or manicured lawn. They have exchanged the "I'm not weeding enough 'guilt'" for the "I need to mow the lawn "guilt.'"

And then there is the newest crop of gardeners that has sprung up out of slick magazines and from being advised to get back to earth. I think some just yearn for an excuse to use and wear their newly acquired gardening paraphernalia and wardrobe.

Perhaps the urge to regain the elemental can not be thwarted even in our age, as it twists and turns and pushes its way to the surface like a tender shoot through pavement. Few endeavors get much more basic and fulfilling than teasing a few precious life-giving nutrients out of the earth with your own two hands.

In a way, gardening makes human beings a much more reliable and renewable resource. In the prehistoric past, those who first learned how to do it with skill and success helped secure the survival of their kind. Not to put in a few tomato plants and a row of string beans feels like a betrayal of all that good groundwork laid so long ago.

Civilization

The Poor Get Poorer and the Rich Get Horses

A lot of less-than-rich people stay that way by trying to afford horses. I did not know this until our horse, which we had kept inexpensively for the past 15 years and mostly unridden for the past five, died.

After an appropriate mourning period my wife started to get interested in riding again. And I encouraged her. It is a good healthy outdoor sport that will make your cheeks pink winter and summer, so what's the harm. Now we are receiving a near-constant stream of packages, from demo jumping saddles (our old saddle was strictly for riding on flat ground) to an assortment of clothing, headgear, and various other supplies from on-line companies. And we don't even have a horse yet, we just lease one.

I, of course, in my customary naiveté, had no idea how the price and scope of horse-related merchandise had grown in the last decade. Sheltered in my make-ends-meet, frugal mentality, I would never have believed the cost of animal paraphernalia could frighten me so much.

At my wife's innocent suggestion we went for a day trip to Manchester, Vermont, last August to watch a giant horse show, which they called a horse festival. The era of moms and pops pulling small Spartan one-or-two-horse trailers is done with. The price of most of the rigs I saw in Manchester would pay off my mortgage.

On a stroll through a vendor's stand at the festival, I noticed a nice shiny bridle and remarked with satisfaction to my wife, "Hey, look, it's only $45." She paused a moment in her thumbing through $300 to $500 riding jackets, (one of which she later bought) to inform me that was not for the whole bridle, just the mouth piece. Huh? Wheeling from that revelation I turned to confront a row of handmade saddles. I sidled up to the nearest one and squinted at the price tag. Let's just say I have bought most of my secondhand cars for less money.

I smiled and insisted we go out and watch the horses.

Horse chic. That's what they should call it. Every item is horse correlated.

99

Sighting By Eye

Off-duty riders wear special lace-up boots and pants with two-tone material in the seat and inner leg. They adorn themselves with only one or two kinds of dogs to go with their horse profile. A Jack Russell terrier or Welsh corgi must be at the end of the leash of any aspiring rider. They seem to like to drive Range Rovers or giant silver SUVs, though I noticed some latitude there. Big flashy American-made pickups with dual wheels in the back were also prized for their utilitarian qualities.

We watched as a teenage girl dismounts after a competition. Instead of walking the horse to the stable herself to look after it, I noticed a man in workman's attire was instantly at her side and took the reins. Just another accoutrement.

Last week we went to West Springfield, Massachusetts, for a big equine event at the Eastern States Exposition. We could barely walk in the building, the place was so packed with horse gear and horse-gear consumers: Everything you can think of for horses and the people who sit on them.

The niches for market focus are such that one vendor carried just the add-on double-sided zipper strips you can zip between the existing zipper teeth on your chaps (leather half-pants you wear over riding pants) to make them fit better as you age and gain girth as a mature rider. This idea would help a lot of middle-aged men save on pants, except that the average pair of new chaps cost, about $300, which makes it a better buy for middle-aged riders than mere middle-aged eaters.

To celebrate not buying anything else at the sprawling equine event I acquiesced and we both purchase matching $44.95 Ariat horse-motif belts made in China. These belts buckle by fastening a silver clip into a silver ring. Her's is black and mine is brown. I don't really know the significance of her color choice versus mine, but perhaps subconsciously I know I won't be in the black very long if this keeps up and I'd better get good at shoveling the brown.

On the inside of our matching belts there is a horse-related phrase embossed in leather. It says: "My goal in life is to be the kind of person my horse thinks I am."

How do you say tight-wad in a whinny.

Civilization

Sighting By Eye

Hanging Outside the Gallery

The police officer on the mountain bike calls out: "you can't hang there."

At the back door of the Mystic Art Association along the river four youths stir slightly as if ruffled by a spring breeze, but nobody has moved yet. The bike patrol swings his two-wheeler in a nonchalant circle and draws alongside the loitering crew.

I note the officer's updated usage, the slang "hanging." In my day it was hanging out, but decades have passed and the "out" is out. "Hanging" all by itself is in. Succinct, in vogue, sign of the times. Even the police have been absorbed, re-routed in the language.

Finally roused, the teenagers get to their feet. They are not frightened into submission, but move grudgingly like a herd used to being prodded into action. The officer straddles his bike and chats with them for a few minutes. Then everyone disperses and the gallery's back lawn reverts to solitude. Just Ted, the mason, and I, building a stone wall around the patio.

Later in the afternoon a pair of black-booted apparitions clank by across the gallery's other patio bound for the same backdoor foyer landing. Two young men clad in more metal than a medieval knight's chain mail come to a halt by the door. They have chain links sprouting and rattling all over their bodies and I think rings and other flesh piercing items hanging wherever possible. They have their hair spiked to a crest that reminds me of a rooster's comb. Ted whispers, "some of them use Elmer's Glue to get it to stand up like that."

I wince at what they have put themselves through. If only they could experience the liberation of less demanding styles.

When I happen by, one of them speaks to me in an innocent voice, just to make conversation. I am as surprised as Hamlet to hear the boyish ghost speak: "to tell the secrets of my prison house I could a tale unfold, whose lightest word would harrow up thy soul." What prison house these two young men occupy between their earrings is not known to me. The afternoons are a busy parapet

102

Civilization

behind the gallery with its meandering path and benches overlooking the river.

Another day there are two high-school-age girls sitting blissfully in the grass within easy earshot. Their voices carry in the fragrant air amidst the scent of blossoming flowers. Presently I hear a string of obscenities drift out of their mouths, served up in very natural and conversational tones. I would have anticipated it in a men's locker room, but then again, maybe not. I am disappointed more than shocked.

While we work laying our stones and mortaring them into the wall, people keep arriving. They come to stroll, to sit, to talk, to take in the scene along the water behind the gallery. They are all "hanging" in one respect or another. Even for the common manual laborer, like me, the back of the gallery screens out the hurried pace on the street side out front.

The young and old who escape to this place have stepped through a little rift. They have found an eddy where the mean current takes a holiday. But soon all must turn and go back, the path is only so long and so winding. Be it the bike patrol or mortgage or other necessity, something sends us all away. When we finish this wall we too will be put into exile.

I visit whenever I have the chance to see how our handiwork wears. It still stands straight. I like to see it and remember hanging with Teddy.

Sighting By Eye

No One Is Standing By the Old Standbys

My Vermont connection called the other night needing a favor. He wanted me to check up on a used carburetor for his 1968, four-cylinder International gas tractor: part number 3414.

I checked, and Crouch's Used Tractor Parts in Lebanon did not have a serviceable replacement. I had barely got out the words "thirty-four-fourteen" when Crouch Junior was already shaking his head. "I can rebuild it," he said. "I can make the parts."

Easy for him to say, but what about the other things in life that wear out and aren't replaceable—because they just don't make them anymore, anywhere, and can't no matter what.

It took me 40 years to discover the best work boot I ever saw, the Chippewa model 60-60. Trouble is, after buying three pairs I learned that despite decades of service and popularity, they had discontinued the model. I think they just wanted to jack up the price and they knew they couldn't get away with it unless they jazzed up the look and design of the thing. Once they made the changes and raised the price—guess what? They didn't sell. Because it wasn't the same great work boot anymore.

Similarly, I found that L.L. Bean carried a line of work pants that wears like iron—

Civilization

black canvas carpenter pants, they called them. I bought three pair and wore them for a year of hard service. When the time came to replace them, I visited the main store in Freeport, Maine, expecting to replenish my supply. I was told by a man in the pants department that he'd never heard of them.

Fortunately a woman in the same department thought otherwise and coaxed a few remaining pairs up on the computer screen. They had been discontinued, but a few languished in the warehouse. I ordered them on the spot.

This is not an aberration.

The old standbys are not being stood by any longer.

Chippewa was bought out by another boot company in recent years and perhaps they wanted a more exciting work boot for today's more exciting customers. They think we get bored with good products that last too long.

And L.L. Bean is changing faster than you can say "Gum Rubber Maine Hunting Shoe," which is probably the only thing they haven't changed in 50 years. The name of the back of the boot has already been modified though; the word "hunting" has been exorcised. The label on the back heel of the boot now says simply "Bean Boots." The word "hunting" must have become a liability.

In some cases it took our parents' or grandparents' generation a lifetime to settle on the products and brand names they would come to trust. There seemed to be a bond established. But counting on continuity is risky business for today's consumer. And probably a real hard sell in the board room as well.

My Vermont connection is skeptical and resourceful. When I called him with the bad news, he said he'd already fixed the carburetor himself. He was just sending out feelers to a fickle world, I suspect.

He is no slave to fashion, but knows the rest of us are.

Sighting By Eye

Mortality

Sighting By Eye

Mortality

A Teacher Wherever You Find Him

I had no idea I had learned anything from him until he died. It was while digging his grave that I realized he had been my teacher all along. He was a simple and solid being who never spoke a word, but communicated his true and stalwart nature solely by his actions.

He was a deep vessel of obedience and patience, especially in his later years, and through my commands, good and bad, I can now see reflected in the life we gave him our own successes and failures.

He was our 13-year-old Labrador Retriever named Bronson.

He couldn't walk in the end, his hips were so bad. Add to that a heart condition that could have killed him at any moment and a cancerous tumor the size of an orange on his spleen. He did not whimper or whine. He wagged his tail from the prone position, even on the day he died.

Determined to make a good grave for him I dug deep and wide through roots and rocks of all sizes in the woods behind our house. A large stone unearthed while digging reminded me of his big brown head and became his headstone. It was two solid hours of work with shovel and crow bar. It was ample time to pass through many layers of soil and grief.

A quick, easy grave might not have given the opportunity to reflect on what a noble dog he was, with few bad habits and many redeeming qualities. Simply put, he was a pillar of our family whose life spanned the childhood of our sons, and I did not comprehend his value until he was gone.

So ingrained in my psyche was his presence, that on the morning after he died I thought I caught the movement of his large brown body emerging from his doghouse out of the corner of my eye.

He used to be good to go on walks with, until his heart condition stopped that two years ago. In the curtailing of his own life's pleasures I could feel a murmur of what all our lives come down to. But the message was not deprivation or sadness; it was more like rolling with the punches. I sensed that in him. He lounged in the sun when he could find it, and he

109

Sighting By Eye

snuggled in the straw of his doghouse when the wind blew.

He became enamored with our warm walkout basement, a place where he would spend the coldest nights curled up at the bottom of the stairs not too far from the wood stove. I think he liked to listen to the kids moving about on the floor above him.

And that's where he died, with his family close by.

When the snow finally fell last week after a fitful winter, I marveled at the stillness of the woods around his grave. A thousand glimpses of his nonchalant self prancing through summer grass extinguished themselves in an instant of that stillness.

But his memory also rekindled warmth in the next heartbeat because he was once here among us trying to show us what love and devotion were all about.

The lesson may be over, but the learning continues. And that is the mark of a good teacher.

Mortality

You Can't Fish in the Same Ocean Twice

I don't know if it's that my end is much closer than my beginning, or just that I feel comfortable and happy revisiting old habits and haunts, but when I hit the half century mark I started pulling out everything from B&W Converse High-top sneakers to my father's old surfcasting rods and Mitchell reels.

Today, after seeing a bubbly 30-something couple land a striped bass on the sand near Watch Hill, I had an incredible urge to put that 1960s vintage surfcasting outfit back into service.

Except that, like the late Frank Sinatra said, I'll be "doing it my way," thanks. Though the glamorous bass fishing sequence was a catalyst to the spirit, it was a debacle to witness. The scene was one that would make an old surfcaster roll in his grave, or at least bob up and down.

Straight out of a summer outdoor sporting catalog in both clothing and physique, this male and female team were casting out live eels into the surf in what I first thought was idle entertainment. That's until they hooked a striped bass. The beachgoers within eye shot broke into applause as the fish was brought ashore, and a mob rushed out to "ooh and ah" over the fish. Suddenly cameras materialized and everybody got their picture taken with the gasping bass. If they were going to eat it, fine, but I had no doubt this crowd was strictly "catch and release." Finally when I thought the fish had been hoisted into the air and breaded with beach sand enough to suffocate it, the woman and man turned on their heels and rushed it back to the water, apparently in the nick of time.

Moments later when she reached her blanket, not far from ours, I heard the female angler talking loudly on her cell phone the way you talk to your hard-of-hearing grandfather. She bubbled on and on about the fish, gushing about its size and so on. "I just wanted to tell you we caught the striped bass," she said again, like she had unwittingly snared the essence of nature or a Holy Grail of the sea. Which she had of course, but the cell phone betrayed

111

Sighting By Eye

Mortality

her. Perhaps without such devices ideas would stay in the mind long enough to make something of themselves. But with such instant communications our minds are now mere conduits, way stations for our thoughts between conception and verbalization, launched and lost immature into the ether or into someone else's ear where they vanish like vapor.

Anyway, I would not look so good catching a bass on the beach, no matter what, no matter the cost. First I would be terribly embarrassed if a crowd of bikini-clad ladies applauded. My father never fished among sunbathers. He usually fished at night all alone with only a small boy in tow. There was the glistening of moonlight on the ocean and the rhythmic roll of the breakers. The soft whine of the line out of the reel and then the click of the bailer going over at the end of the cast.

It was an art performed by work-weary and weather-beaten outdoorsmen and a few sporting ladies. You fished in high rubber boots called waders. There was an unspoken and silent camaraderie among fishermen, and the sport had not been co-opted by art directors and accessorized into oblivion by marketers. My father wore a T-shirt, which was actually underwear, and old Khaki work pants. He had a big-billed fishing hat and no nonsense International Scout with an all-metal dashboard and manual lock-out hubs to get him there. It was a no-frill sport practiced by a guy who ate what he caught.

I have no idea why watching those folks catch that striped bass today was so troubling to my old memories. But then I recalled something that happened decades ago.

Every day for years my father wore blue denim overalls to his job in construction work. I'm sure he loved them with their rugged utility and durability. Then in the 1960s hippies started wearing them as a kind of unofficial uniform. Overnight, my father stopped wearing his overalls and never wore them again.

Every generation wants its own way.

Sighting By Eye

Mortality

A Little Landscaping for the Soul

A couple of weeks ago we went to a memorial service for a man I had never met. I only began to get to know him on the way to the service.

My oldest son, age 16, surprised us by getting dressed in his best clothes and wanting to come with us on that Saturday afternoon.

I asked my son on the ride to Eastford: "What was he like?" My son shrugged from the backseat, not knowing how to answer such an unspecific question. I rephrased: "Was he a big guy?" My son often admires big strapping men who operate heavy machinery and talk like ex-Marines.

"No," he said, "he wasn't a big guy."

"Was he a tough guy?" I persisted. "No," he answered again. "He was kind of soft-spoken," he added, in a way that told me he was thinking back to his encounters with the man.

Over the years, my son had met the man many times while out on loam deliveries with my father-in-law, whose business put him in contact with Gene often. Gene had been a landscaper. He spread loam and generally made things beautiful down in southeastern Connecticut.

Like me, my wife had also never met Gene, but she had talked to him from time to time on the phone over the last five years. Gene had a form of blood cancer, and like my wife had had a stem cell transplant. She had offered encouragement and some of her experience. I remember him calling, her talking.

The church in Eastford was old, bone white, and sat on a hill at the outskirts of town. Down to the last detail, things were well kept. Not a trace of extravagance, just New England practicality. The old wood pews looked fresh painted, white with a maroon trim. An organist belted out hymns before and during the service on an enormous instrument built into the sanctuary front wall. Its tall pipes shone clean and sounded clear.

In the vestibule where the attendees gathered in clusters before the service was a table and wall display of Gene's life. There were photos of him

115

Sighting By Eye

doing the things we do in our lives. One photo of him stood out from the hustle and bustle of the rest of the portfolio. It was of him sitting contently looking up at the camera. I would guess his wife took that photo. On the table were his work gloves, a pair of wire-frame glasses, and a tattered baseball cap.

That a man could be summed up by such a modest inventory made me uneasy. But it only turned out to be evidence of larger accomplishment.

At a point in the memorial those in attendance were invited, if they chose, to say a few words about the deceased. I have seen this before and the results vary. When the offer was tendered, there were a few moments of silence while we waited. I did not know if the quiet was prologue or postscript. Then beginning like a barely perceptible landslide, the earth began to move. First spoke a man from Waterford, who had not seen Gene in years, but who by chance had heard about his passing and had driven all that way on a rainy November day. He said he would not be where he is in life today if it hadn't been for Gene.

Another went up, then another, and another. On they came. Some lost their composure, sputtered, wiped tears away, some spoke in a steady resolve, knowing what they owed and trying to make amends. They spoke about how much of himself Gene was willing to give. How much he loved to talk. How he loved to work outdoors and make flower beds and yards beautiful. They spoke about how happy he was just driving to work, that unbelievable 50 miles or more each way to work everyday, down by the ocean. There is no freeway door-to-door between Eastford and Essex. It's meandering back roads, stop signs, and an occasional traffic light.

One fit, middle-aged woman with a thick shock of white hair stood up and spoke about how on a landscaping job she introduced Gene, whom she worked with, to her niece visiting from Texas. That was five years ago and after he was diagnosed with his disease. The niece and Gene fell in love and were married.

There was no body in the church that day. Whatever they had done with Gene had been done.

All that remained were so many people thankful to have known him and his hat with the brim frayed beyond reason.

116

A Game for the Ages on the Fenway

Torrential rains were forecast. But the evening is dry so far.

The road is a tangle of concrete launching ramps that propel you only to the next red light. The Boston drivers all around us perform brazen acts that make bullfighting look like a parlor sport.

The game starts at 7:05 just off the fen. My Irish-American guide gestures toward the Charles River and the wet lowlands at its banks. "That's why they call it Fen way," he says, matter-of-fact.

Company does make the difference. Seen through his eyes, the consummate Sox fan, the evening has a jewel-like quality, singular, like it has been performed 10,000 times for the first time—the crowd getting seated, the worn passageways coming to life, the young men moving around on the groomed infield dirt. Fenway Park looks like an old green jewelry box, small and antique, sandwiched into a city.

The night is a good one for the Boston Red Sox. Also good for my guide and our sons. The final score is 5 to 3 Boston. Fenway hotdogs, popcorn, soda, baseball hats, the works.

We even sat between the dugout and home plate about six rows back until the rightful owners of the seats showed up an inning and a half into the game. It was all done with proper etiquette, we relinquishing without batting an eye and the latecomers were assured warm seats.

But the game did look different from the bleachers. The ball carried strangely in the lights, drifting up and out. But the fans in the hinterland seemed happy in their realm. Earthy participants in the game of life, beer, off-color cheers, in some senses closer to the game than their erudite cousins 400 feet closer to home plate. Whereas in the pricey section a pleasant anonymity or friendly nod was exchanged between seatmates, in the bleachers, good-natured shouts of "down in front" and improvised chest-thumping cheers cemented the bond.

The pace of the game was brisk, journeyman-like. The infield surgeons

117

Sighting By Eye

Mortality

catching and throwing like a million bucks, true to their salaries. The out-fielders tight like a spring and then off like a shot, eating up turf toward the falling sphere. What a game. Fudged by novices, maligned by cynics, executed with grace by these young men.

And therein lay the rub. I must confess I recognized the name of only one of the players on the field and that only in passing. But late in the game a figure appeared in the bull pen just below us in the bleachers. Could it be?

The same pitcher that pitched the last time I came to Fenway 16 years ago was warming up. Among all the anonymous faces on the field was one I recognized. The same mustache, the same long hair trailing out the back of his cap. The same springy gait. Alleluia. Maybe creased and gnarled a shade or two, but lean and fit. A man who kept himself up.

Out onto the field trotted Dennis Eckersley. It was only for two outs, but for me it capped the evening. I watched his pitches zip to the plate. The leg up, the arm over. The same Eckersley, the same number 43 on his back, now a number close to his age.

I had been away from the heart of New England for an awfully long time. Away from that radio in the dark room off the kitchen crackling with Carl Yastremski and George Scott, Dwight Evans and Louis Tiant, my father's eyes closed, listening, easy chair tilted back. It felt like home.

The rain waited and let only a sprinkle fall in the ninth to remind us it could have ruined our sport. Such an ephemeral game, a game of youth, quick as a passing summer shower in the scheme of things.

On the way home it poured and poured and poured. "Maybe this year," whispered the mantra.

Sighting By Eye

Losing Lieutenant Morrow

I went to a funeral last week for an old lady I knew.

Talking about her, the priest mentioned her years of service. For a split second I didn't know what he meant, and then of course realized he was referring to her service as a nurse. Which got me thinking about what a nurse amounts to.

When I was a young boy, Marion was the nurse at my family doctor's office on Gravel Street in Mystic for 12 years.

A nurse's only work, it seems to me, is helping to care for people. There might be a couple of ancillary tasks, but the primary function of a nurse is humanity and its well-being.

How few jobs in this world revolve around such a simple and exalted function—healing. Doctors do it too, but it seems to me most of them are like generals in the Army; they understand the art of making war on disease but serve at some little distance by necessity. A nurse toils in the bloody trenches, armed with bedpans and clean towels, a foot soldier against illness that knocks us down.

Three pews ahead of me in the church were three ladies. I had never seen them before but I knew they were nurses at a nurse's funeral. There was a purpose about the way they moved. I didn't see three doctors in any of the pews.

A few years back, I was having some pains and asked retired nurse Marion about it. She prodded me in the lower back around the kidney and asked a question or two. Usually brisk in manner, she dropped her sergeant's demeanor, even though she had been a lieutenant, and slipped into the role of comforting healer seamlessly—she must have done so countless times. I felt know-how in her touch and straightaway she eased my mind toward the road of recovery.

She was an officer in the Army Nurses' Corps during World War II. Someone told me she treated veterans after they came back from overseas wounded.

120

Mortality

As it turned out, the same day Marion died I went to the cinema and saw the movie *Saving Private Ryan*. Veterans have said the movie does a pretty good job of depicting the terror and chaos of combat. But telling such a raw truth so well about one aspect, it becomes difficult to do much of anything else—like tell a story. Or maybe the story was only that war is tragedy surrounded by accident and irony.

"You can't win," was a favorite saying of Marion's. She used to toss it out like a dud hand grenade at the end of nearly every conversation she had with you. Despite her "you can't win" lament, Marion stood up for whatever she believed in, hell or high water, not concerned with winning or losing it seemed. Perhaps she was just a guarded optimist who wanted to hedge her bets, knowing in the end no one gets out alive.

I didn't see a single tear on the cheeks of the three nurses at church, but in their countenance and bearing they gave one fine accounting of their fallen comrade in arms. We all, in the pews, had passed another mile marker in some personal war on our march toward eternity. Knowing like Lieutenant Morrow always told us, to the last man and nurse, you can't win, but you can make a pretty good life trying.

Sighting By Eye

Mortality

Passing Through Some Deep Uncharted Place

Their 72-foot lobster boat vanished on November 21, 1989. Days later I shoveled out a stall, my breath white vapor blasts in the November air. I thought of those five fishermen out there somewhere.

We couldn't escape knowing they were still with us. Three hundred miles from this Stonington farm they saw flares go off two nights running in the late autumn sky. But the sea is so big and men so small.

The next day I shoveled again out the door facing southeast, and in my mind's eye saw that great curtain of imperious cold spread like sheet steel across the North Atlantic. The Coast Guard planes were up again last night, but no more flares.

None the next night, or the next. None ever again.

Finally, in December at St. Marys in the sea village there was a memorial service for them. I saw my friend that morning, just before he went to church for the funeral without bodies.

Everything seemed so normal. He'd been a fisherman once and an artist. I never doubted he had something in common with those men lost from the *Heidi Marie*. I just never thought he would become lost with them.

Three years have passed. During that span I saw him only twice. Closed up in his house, frail, a whisper of his former robust self, he said he thought of dying. Last week I saw my friend again. He was almost his old self, but he seemed to have been adrift.

It hurt me. Not just to see him that way, but more selfishly, it made me afraid. A man with a sharp lust for life had suddenly turned to ashes. I didn't want to see him. I had put off visiting him.

In the cold North Atlantic, crammed in a survival suit and cramped in a small covered raft, what is it like when they can't find the source of your flares and the cold won't stop?

Is there a time, any time near the end, when the world looks different. Despair you'd expect. Total despair. But can it leave room for anything else?

123

Sighting By Eye

Can God climb aboard with you for the last leg of the journey?

My friend must have been sending up flares too. Silent, invisible ones. On an errand, after not seeing him for more than a year, I stopped by. He was standing in the bright light of the kitchen window. And he caught up my hand and the grip was solid.

We talked. We went into his studio. He had had a birthday three days before, his 85th. He was frail, but his eyes held the mark. Together we looked through drawing after drawing, painting after painting. In awe of the strength and raw beauty of the work, he said again and again, "I can't believe I did this."

It was clear he was looking back. He said to me he would paint no more.

I suspect for some reason unknown to me he had passed through some deep uncharted place since the *Heidi Marie* sank. And in some minute but powerful way he had swept me along with him.

The man in the raft can not fight the cold forever. He may rest his head in a comrade's arms and be in awe and peace for a while. Only he will never be the same again.

Like my friend.

Mortality

Knowing What Boat to Choose

I enter the old barn with rain pounding outside. The huge, quiet, dry room is cluttered on the floor, but the roof is so high and long the space feels airy. A handful of windows high up don't make it bright, but you can see clearly in all but the far corners. On the floor, turned upside down like a giant turtle shell, is the hull of an unfinished boat. The reason I came here.

You have to know how to time a boat project with the tide your own life takes. Though he'd built others before it, the man who built this unfinished boat died before this one was done. The new owner bought it with the property and thought at first he would tackle it, but to his credit realized it was too much and will let it go.

This boat is not a season's work. It is not a year's work even. It could be the work of a lifetime. I crawl underneath and stare up at the hundreds of laminated seams and see in it the hundreds of hours of a man's life fastened as well there. The template forms still fill the inside of the boat, but outside the hull is smooth and beautiful, already sanded fair. A date on the outside of the stem says 1973. This boat has been poised here for more than 30 years waiting to be finished. Would I be the proper custodian of this commitment, I wonder.

When my offspring were small a friend of my wife's family gave them intricate ship models made from plastic kits as gifts. There were three or four in all, and all except one were wrecked on the shoals of children's rough play. The rigging became tangled and askew on the masts, and tiny plastic parts broke off until the ships looked as if they had gone through a typhoon. Not until I went to the man's funeral did I think about all the hours near the end of his life he siphoned off for those models, but it was too late to save them, except one which we kept on a high shelf and out of reach of little hands. I can only hope he built them as toys, not monuments.

I have found some people like to work on boats and some people like to go out in boats. Personally I like a combination of the two with the emphasis

Sighting By Eye

Mortality

distinctly not on work. Of course working on a boat can be like play if it is enjoyed. I once heard John Kelly (the younger), Boston Marathon winner, say that play is defined as self-directed activity. But it is quite possible to self-direct too much activity until it becomes drudgery. I have restored one small boat and another awaits my pleasure at this moment, scheduled loosely for when time and inclination permit.

Some people are constantly getting involved with more projects than they can handle. They become activity junkies and meet themselves coming and going until their bodies and minds are destroyed prematurely. I don't think the builder of this boat was like that. From the rest of the place I get the feeling that the man simply had a methodical and time-consuming passion for boats, and time ran out.

There is a finite trajectory to boat ownership. Only the Vikings were buried in their boats. I look at this big unfinished boat in the barn and I have serious doubts. Even my wife has laid down the gauntlet: I must sell two boats out of the five I own to acquire another. But I think I can navigate around that by selling one boat and one outboard motor. But that is not the point.

I stop at Hamburg Cove on the Connecticut River on the way home and walk around in the downpour looking at the eclectic collection of watercraft there to see what the barn boat could become. In a cold rain in November you begin to realize that your days and your boats are ultimately, in the end, numbered.

So choose carefully. You mustn't make a bargain with a boat you cannot keep.

Sighting By Eye

Some of the Ties That Bind Us

My 12-year-old son met me at the door the other day with a grim look on his face. I knew something was wrong.

"Something really bad happened today," he said in a monotone, accompanied by a sad face.

I thought he must have got into trouble at school and I started to shake my head and say how he should be more responsible—when he cut me off with words that were no more than a whisper.

"My teacher died," he managed to get out.

I knew who it would be, because one of his teachers had been ill for quite a while.

He said the name, confirming it.

The teacher was quite a "character" as they used to say. I only saw him a couple of times; once at open house and then much later in the school year while I waited in the office to collect my son for an early dismissal.

At that middle school open house I saw a vast and colorful tie collection in that teacher's room, along with all kinds of interesting things and displays. And it was obvious my son enjoyed the eccentricities of this teacher, such as his playing golf in the halls of the school, and I'm sure other incorrigible bits of good fun I have no idea of.

The day after the teacher died most of his students wore a tie to school. Not with dress shirts of course, but just around their necks with whatever they usually wear to middle school in springtime. My son came into the bedroom at about 6:30 a.m. asking me for a tie and the help to put it on.

We dug out an old patriotic model with the stars and strips on it and I had to put it on myself to try to remember how to tie it on another person. The school, I heard that day, was full of kids wearing ties.

The last time I saw the teacher was in the school office and I came close to speaking to him, but did not. At first I wasn't sure who it was, because he had lost so much weight. He had pulled out a pink slip of paper from his mailbox

128

Mortality

and was analyzing it. He made a joke to the secretary about being fired or laid off, but of course he was not; it was probably just one of those pink "while you were out" pad notes. It struck me then as a tinge of gallows humor on his part, but if it really was I have no way of knowing. But I did know he was living with cancer that had spread to his bones. So I couldn't help thinking on some level he meant in a wry Shakespearian way that if he was dismissed, he would be dismissed by a much higher authority than the Board of Ed.

I could have asked him then about my son's progress in class and probably would have got a very thorough and honest answer. But for some reason, I did not. I wish I had done that now. I wish I had taken something from him, and given my engagement and interest.

My son went to the funeral and then to the cemetery yesterday. He told me the church was packed with students wearing ties—bright colorful and wild ties—just like the tie collection he had been famous for in his classroom.

And for the first time I can remember, my son spoke about death in a way that told me he knows he is mortal.

"Every man is a piece of the continent, a part of the main," said John Donne.

It occurs to me we often forget that.

Donne's poem continues: "any man's death diminishes me, because I am involved in mankind"

My son's teacher was involved until the very end—he stopped by school just a few days before he passed away—to check on, I think, the ties that bind us.